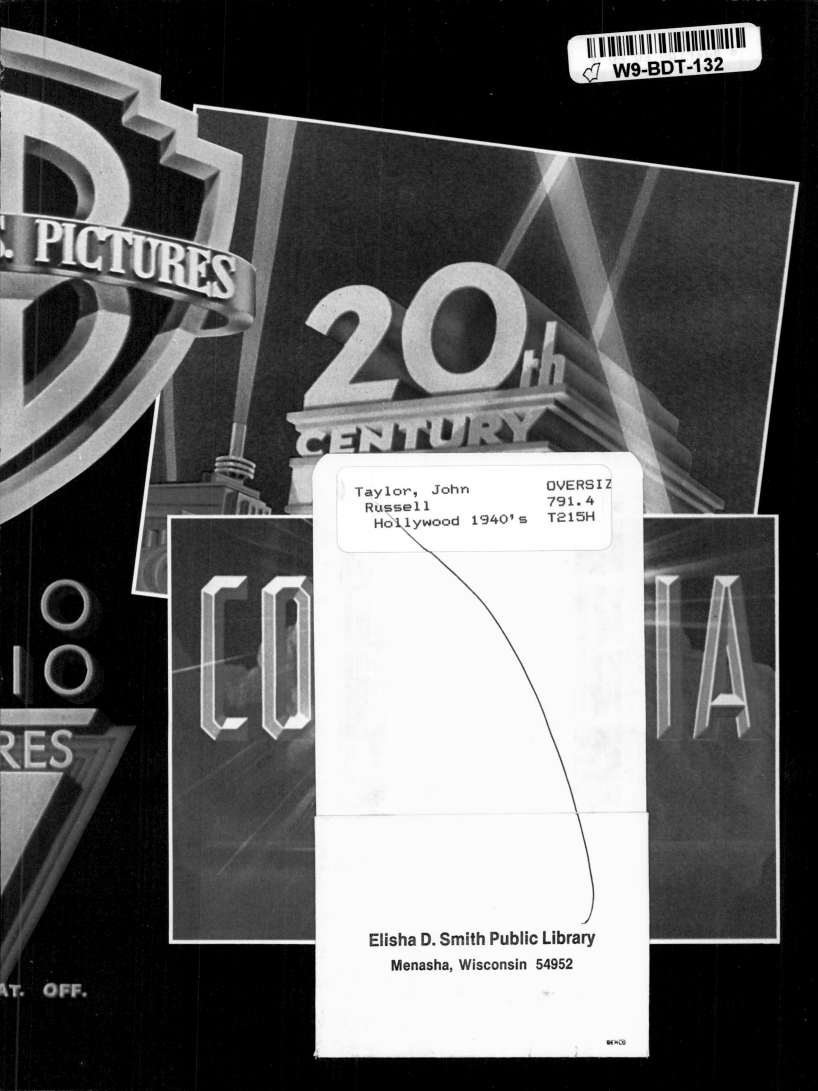

Hollywood 1940s

Hollywood 1940s

John Russell Taylor

GALLERY BOOKS

This book was devised and produced by
Multimedia Publications (UK) Ltd.

Editor: Richard Rosenfeld
Assistant editor: Sydney Francis
Production: Arnon Orbach
Design: Michael Hodson Designs
Picture Research: Vivien Adelman

First published in the United States of America 1985 by Gallery
Books, an imprint of W.H. Smith Publishers Inc., 112 Madison
Avenue, New York, NY 10016

ISBN 0 8317 4521 5

Typeset by Letterspace Ltd.
Origination by DS Colour International Ltd., London
Printed in Italy by Sagdos

Contents

Left: *George Raft, Ida Lupino and Humphrey Bogart are rudely interrupted in* **They Drive by Night** *(1948).*

Page 1: *Private eye Groucho Marx discovers why men have been following Marilyn Monroe in* **Love Happy** *(1949).*

Pages 2-3: *Monty Woolley and the "oomph girl" Ann Sheridan in* **The Man Who Came to Dinner** *(1941).*

Endpapers: *Each Hollywood studio had its own distinctive logo.*

The Business of War 1940-1

Chapter 1

The time-honored tradition of dividing trends and movements in the cinema into decades is essentially a matter of convenience. In the forties, all aspects of life were dictated by the decade's momentous political events – rather than the arbitrary notion of a contained timespan existing between 1940 and 1950 – and cinema was no exception.

As far as Hollywood goes, the period we regard as the thirties really starts in 1927 with the coming of sound, contains the greatest era of the studio system, and ends in December 1941 when America became involved in World War II. The forties, for all intents and purposes, begin there – and the film traditions that were established during and after the conflict would dominate until the early fifties, when the McCarthy witch-hunts and the emergence of television changed the shape and flavor of American cinema.

Music and murder

An idea of the forties still persists, but it is too nebulous a tag. The two great screen movements that grew up during the era in Hollywood were the great MGM musical and the dark murder thriller that came to be known as *film noir*. The former really starts with the arrival of producer Arthur Freed at Louis B. Mayer's studio in 1939 and lingers on until the later fifties – a period bookended by Freed's productions of **Babes in Arms** (1939) and **Gigi** (1958). *Film noir* emerged from the shadows of **Citizen Kane** (1941) – the first film directed by Orson Welles, who was the single most important figure to arrive on the film scene since talkies began – and **The Maltese Falcon** (1941), still going in 1953, though its resonances could be felt on into the seventies.

All the same, the forties may have more than accidental significance in the history of Hollywood. The decade's beginning, even before America was forced to declare war on Japan, was marked by an alarming slump in cinema attendance that put an end, forever, to the extravagance that had characterized film-making in the previous ten years. By the year 1950, Hollywood was again in a chastened frame of mind, with the menace of the small screen already apparent, along with the break-up of the old studio empires of production, distribution and exhibition through the strict application of the anti-trust laws.

That makes the forties sound like a pretty miserable decade – and there was another alarming slump in the number of cinema-goers about half way through. By 1946 the studios were obliged to feel their way towards a new definition of audiences and their tastes – which

Right: *The tough private-eye Sam Spade (Humphrey Bogart – left) and the effeminate crook Joel Cairo (Peter Lorre) having second thoughts about smooth-talking Brigid O'Shaughnessy (Mary Astor) in John Huston's* **The Maltese Falcon** *(1941).*

necessarily reflected the emotional impact of the war. In fact, the salient characteristic of Hollywood at this particular time was its extraordinary buoyancy.

There had always been a swiftness in adjusting to new market pressures in Hollywood, but the beginning of the forties required a greater adaptability than had ever been needed before. Although the war that had started in Europe on 3 September 1939 must have seemed remote from Hollywood concerns, the European market still mattered very much. In the late thirties, Hitler's invasion of Austria and Czechoslovakia had caused a significant drop in the revenues for Hollywood films from those countries. The outbreak of war made the whole commercial scene in Europe more impenetrable still. The

Left: *Sam Spade (Humphrey Bogart) about to hand over murderess Brigid O'Shaughnessy to the law in **The Maltese Falcon** (1941). Bebe Daniels (1931) and Bette Davis (1936) had previously played Brigid.*

Below: *Karin Blake (Greta Garbo) recovers from an evening of playing her own imaginary glamorous twin sister Katrin in **Two-Faced Woman** (1941). Ruth Ellis (Ruth Gordon) tends to her.*

contraction of the home market – with profits for 1940 almost a third less than those of 1939 (when **Gone With the Wind** was the chief attraction) also needed to be curtailed.

Alone at last

The first victims of this period of transition were two of the gems in MGM's crown. Greta Garbo, Hollywood's supreme "love goddess", had been appreciated more enthusiastically in Europe than in America for the previous few years. Arriving in Hollywood from Sweden with her mentor the director Mauritz Stiller, in 1925, Garbo had moved through the silent era and the first ten years of talkies as a gloomy, tempest-tossed woman made radiantly divine by camera-man William Daniels in such films as Clarence Brown's **Flesh and the Devil** (1926), **Anna Christie** (1930) and **Anna Karenina** (1935), Edmund Goulding's **Love** (1927) and **Grand Hotel** (1932), and George Cukor's **Camille** (1936). But to stay at the top she had to lose her remoteness – the very thing that made her a star – and her grand airs, and be remade closer to the hearts of middle America. She was still glacial, but less so, in Ernst Lubitsch's **Ninotchka** (1939), "the film that made Garbo laugh", and then MGM came up with Cukor's **Two-Faced Woman** (1941), which turned her into a

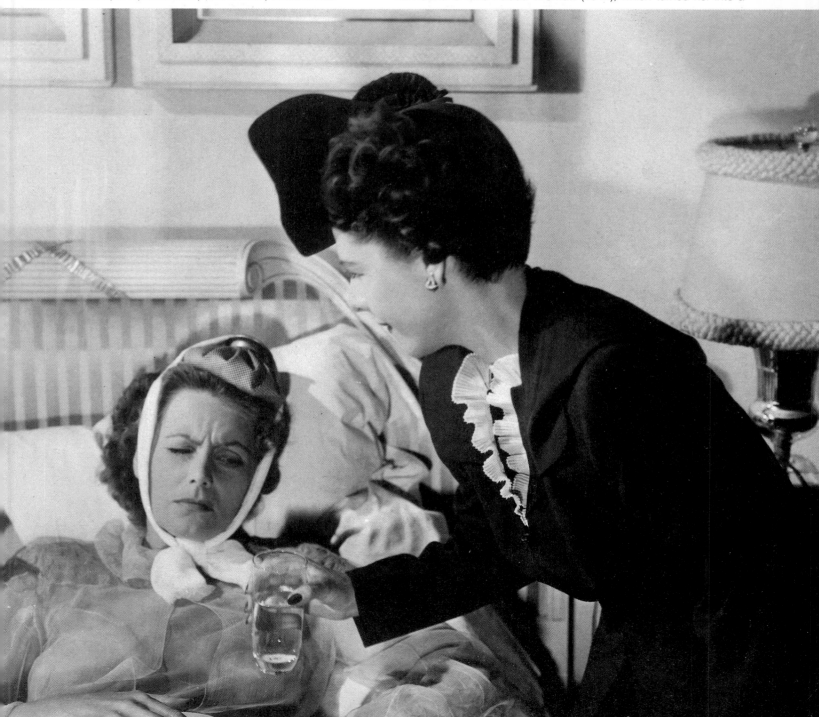

neglected American wife bent on getting even with her philandering husband by posing as her own more glamorous double. She wore a swimsuit and introduced a dance novelty called the Choka-Chika – all to no avail. Voluntarily she retired from movies, and never came back – a move that preserved her stardom forever.

It is significant that Garbo's great rival through the thirties, Marlene Dietrich, would leave behind her the mists and shadows that her director Josef von Sternberg had wreathed around her on Paramount's sound stages in six masterpieces of eroticism – including **Morocco** (1930), **Shanghai Express** (1932) and **The Devil Is a Woman** (1935) – and, from the late thirties, find herself in the more accessible world of Westerns, including **Destry Rides Again** (1939) and **The Spoilers** (1942), and lighter romances, dramas or comedies. Other than that, she was a tireless entertainer of the troops overseas.

MGM's other major casualty at this time was the light-operatic duo of Nelson Eddy and Jeannette MacDonald, the stars of such saccharine vehicles as **Naughty Marietta** (1935) and **The Girl of the Golden West** (1938). As with Garbo, a newer American look was required for the fashion-conscious forties and so they graduated to a Rodgers and Hart score with **I Married an Angel** (1942). And that was the end of another long and successful run.

Tried and tested

These were the most dramatic of a series of similar quick and perhaps precipitate decisions to try and alter the stars' profiles. Though war and the loss of European markets had affected Garbo's and MacDonald and Eddy's popularity, it is very likely that changing tastes would have diminished the box-office receipts from their films anyway. On the whole, thirties-style movies and stars still dominated the scene at the beginning of the forties. Well-upholstered biopics, swashbuckling costume epics, screwball comedies, highly wrought melodramas for important female stars – all these were still around and very popular with moviegoers.

Right: *Queen Elizabeth I (Flora Robson) is won over by Captain Geoffrey Thorpe (Errol Flynn), who is scheming to plunder the galleons of the Spanish Main in* **The Sea Hawk** *(1940). Flora Robson had previously played this royal role in* **Fire Over England** *(1937), with Laurence Olivier and Vivien Leigh among her subjects.*

Left: *Vivien Leigh playing Emma Hamilton to Laurence Olivier's Lord Nelson in Alexander Korda's patriotic* **That Hamilton Woman** *(1941).*
Bottom: *The glamorous Bette Davis playing Regina Giddens in William Wyler's production of* **The Little Foxes** *(1941).*

Below: *A performance of Hamlet in Warsaw being interrupted by the approach of the German invasion in* **To Be or Not to Be** *(1942). Manager Charles Halton is alarmed, but not as much as the actor Joseph Tura (Jack Benny), wondering whether his unfaithful wife Maria (Carole Lombard) can explain away her latest admirer.*

After their success with such socially concerned biographical pictures as **The Story of Louis Pasteur** (1935) and **The Life of Emile Zola** (1937), both directed by William Dieterle and starring Paul Muni, Warner Brothers continued in a similar vein in 1940. That year, Dieterle directed Edward G. Robinson in **The Story of Dr Ehrlich's Magic Bullet** and **A Dispatch From Reuters**. In the first Robinson played the discoverer of a cure for syphilis, a curiously daring choice of subject sanctioned by the Hays Office (the official arbiter of morality and censorship in American films) for its superior taste and message. In the second he played the founder of the famous press agency working his way up in the communications world from humble beginnings with carrier pigeons.

Also at Warners, Errol Flynn, the star of **Captain Blood** (1935) and **The Adventures of Robin Hood** (1938), completed his trio of spectacular swashbucklers for Michael Curtiz with **The Sea Hawk** (1940), made with all the luxurious back-up the studio could muster – sweeping music by Erich Wolfgang Korngold, lavish sets by Anton Grot. A rousing tale of privateers, it was also an ingenious propaganda piece with a strong anti-Nazi message, mainly delivered by Flora Robson as Queen Elizabeth I. Since Hollywood was still bound by an act ensuring the preservation in word and deed of America's neutrality, it was both a bold and cunning film. But otherwise it was the last of its kind; after a couple of Westerns the uneasy Curtiz-Flynn partnership ended and Flynn went into more Westerns and war films for Raoul Walsh, also at Warner Brothers.

Names to conjure with

Meanwhile the other studios essayed Warner-style biopics and social dramas at their peril. By 1940-1 the former was so well established as a successful genre that everyone seemed to be getting in on the act. At MGM it took two films, **Young Tom Edison** and **Edison, the Man** (both 1940), to cover the life of America's all-purpose inventor, who grew up from Mickey Rooney to Spencer Tracy somewhere in between the two movies.

Fox for its part discovered a new swashbuckling star in Tyrone Power, whom Rouben Mamoulian directed with dash and verve in **The Mark of Zorro** (1940) and **Blood and Sand** (1941).

Among all these films made prior to America's entering the war, the strongest propaganda statement was made in Alexander Korda's **That Hamilton Woman** (1941), with Laurence Olivier as Lord Nelson and Vivien Leigh in the title role. It was a brasher, more pro-British, anti-Nazi piece than **The Sea Hawk** – Korda was known to be a close friend of Winston Churchill and it was suspected that he had been sent to Hollywood to carry Britain's fight into American hearts and minds.

The thirties-style melodrama remained in vogue at the beginning of the forties and the reigning female stars were to be found in weepies and women's pictures. Joan Crawford played a hideously scarred, mentally deranged criminal who becomes a new woman after plastic surgery in **A Woman's Face** (1941); Bette Davis played a murderess in **The Letter** and was passionately malicious in **The Little Foxes** (1941); and Vivien Leigh was a ballerina who turns to prostitution in a

Below: *Wealthy Tracy Lord (Katharine Hepburn) in* **The Philadelphia Story** *(1940) having a brief fling with James Stewart before deciding to remarry her first husband, Cary Grant* **right**.

The new comic genius on the horizon was Preston Sturges, a highly successful writer of cynical comedies, who finally bludgeoned Paramount into letting him direct his own scripts. The first results of this, **The Great McGinty** and **Christmas in July** (both 1940), were trial runs, comedies that took a few easy digs at political corruption and the money-ethos without seriously challenging audience expectations. But with **The Lady Eve** (1941), Sturges abandoned social comment in favor of sexual warfare, pitching a wily lady gambler (Barbara Stanwyck) against a moralistic biologist (Henry Fonda) who is more at home with snakes. Sturges' fourth film, **Sullivan's Travels** (1941), about a crusading film-maker who learns the hard way that entertainment means more than messages, was perhaps the funniest film of 1941.

Above: *Comedy-film director (Joel McCrea) sets out to discover real life but finally gets too much of it in **Sullivan's Travels** (1941).*

Right: *Charlie Chaplin, who brilliantly plays both the fascist leader Adenoid Hynkel and the Jewish barber who impersonates him to speak to the world of peace and brotherhood in **The Great Dictator** (1940).*

remake of **Waterloo Bridge** (1940). But Norma Shearer was on her way out, with her stock falling fast in such ill-suited vehicles as the anti-fascist **Escape** (1940) and the stand-by romantic comedy **Her Cardboard Lover** (1942).

Comedy with class

Of the great funny ladies, Carole Lombard, undisputed queen of screwball comedy, appeared in Hitchcock's **Mr and Mrs Smith** (1941) and Ernst Lubitsch's **To Be or Not to Be** (1942) before she was tragically killed in an air crash while on tour selling war bonds. **To Be or Not to Be**, starring Jack Benny as an actor playing Hamlet in occupied Poland and Lombard as his adulterous wife scheming with him against the Germans, is now regarded as a classic of black comedy and an acerbic anti-Nazi piece. Lubitsch, Hollywood's master of sophisticated wit and frothy comedy, had earlier abandoned his usual Ruritanian setting for **The Shop Around the Corner** (1940), a gentle and touching romantic comedy set in an imaginary Budapest department store and matching the comic gifts of the usually tearful Margaret Sullavan with those of James Stewart to charming effect.

Much more in tune with the forties, however, was a film that put Stewart in the fast-talking and bitchy high society of Cary Grant and Katharine Hepburn. It was George Cukor's **The Philadelphia Story** (1940), a comedy of manners sharper and more polished than most Hollywood products of the time.

Screwball comedies were still in vogue. Howard Hawks, who in the forties as in the thirties, tackled most genres with characteristic skill and ease, contributed two excellent entries in **His Girl Friday** (1940), a remake of **The Front Page** (1931) with Cary Grant and Rosalind Russell battling for the headlines, and **Ball of Fire** (1941), with Gary Cooper as one of seven professors surrounding Barbara Stanwyck's stripper Sugarpuss O'Shea. But there was nothing in either of these films to suggest the forties had ushered in any new trends.

Chaplin speaks out

Even in this uneasy period before Hollywood really took stock of the war, it was possible for film-makers to use comedy to comment on the European situation. **To Be or Not to Be** was one mordant example, but the most famous was Charles Chaplin's **The Great Dictator** (1940), his first talkie.

Chaplin was a reluctant convert to sound. He had made only two films in the thirties, **City Lights** (1931) and **Modern Times** (1936). Both were brilliant, but both evaded the new medium. **City Lights** uses sound effects and a musical score but is wordless; **Modern Times**, which saw the last appearance of the little Tramp, is, in fact, a rejection of the new technological age, another silent whose only concession to dialogue is a scene in which Chaplin speaks gibberish.

Below: *Three members of the Joad family, on their way from Oklahoma to California in* **The Grapes of Wrath** *(1940): pregnant Rosasharn (Dorris Bowdon), Ma (Jane Darwell) and Tom (Henry Fonda), just out of prison for homicide. The others* **bottom right** *(from left to right) are Rosasharn's husband Connie (Eddie Quillan), Pa (Russell Simpson), Uncle John (Frank Darien), Al (O. Z. Whitehead) and the itinerant ex-preacher Jim Casy (John Carradine).*
Right: *Joel McCrea, pictured here with Barbara Pepper and Robert Benchley, stars as an American journalist caught up with the Nazis in the Alfred Hitchcock thriller* **Foreign Correspondent** *(1940).*

Dictator of Bacteria). The film made Chaplin's political position very clear and earned him a great deal of criticism. His independence from the studios enabled him to speak freely, but he in particular suffered from the loss of the European intellectual audience his silent comedy had built up. And since he was, though a long time back, an emigré from Britain and had not troubled to hide, either privately or in his films, his left-wing sympathies, he was viewed with suspicion by the Senate committee investigating possible infringements of the Neutrality Act by "inciting to war".

Hitch under suspicion

Alfred Hitchcock was, too. Hitchcock had arrived in Hollywood in 1939 – his greatest years still in front of him. He had quickly mastered the silent film in Britain and had directed one or two films a year through the thirties, building up his familiar world of espionage, murder and suspense in such films as **The Man Who Knew Too Much** (1934), **The Thirty-Nine Steps** (1935) and **The Lady Vanishes** (1938). In America he started with **Rebecca** (1940), a classic of female psychology adapted from Daphne du Maurier's best-selling novel and set in Cornwall, England, and followed it with **Foreign Correspondent** (1940), set in Europe, and (after the matrimonial comedy **Mr and Mrs Smith**) **Suspicion** (1941). It was originally intended that the murder-suspect hero (Cary Grant) of **Suspicion**, a masterful Hitchcock suspense thriller, should go off to redeem himself in the Battle of Britain, but good sense prevailed.

However, Hitchcock was clearly not pleasing the isolationists in America – the real culprit, in their eyes, was **Foreign Correspondent**. Under the guise of another suspense film, this was about spies who might be from anywhere, and showed the political education of one American journalist whose ignorance about Europe gives way to a strongly pro-British and anti-Nazi position. The final scene is an

Prolific during the silent era, Chaplin now spaced his films out by years – there would be only one more from him in the forties, **Monsieur Verdoux** (1947), the story of a Bluebeard murderer. With marital problems and a political smear campaign against him to contend with, it was a difficult decade for Chaplin.

The Great Dictator had him in the dual role of Adenoid Hynkel, Dictator of Tomania, and his double, a little Jewish barber. Fierce in his attack on European fascism, Chaplin satirized not only Hitler, but Goebbels (Henry Daniell as Garbitsch), Goering (Billy Gilbert as Marshall Herring) and Mussolini (Jack Oakie as Benzino Napaloni,

Right: *The publisher of the scurrilous "New York Inquirer", Charles Foster Kane (Orson Welles) and his drama critic (Joseph Cotten) in* **Citizen Kane** *(1941). Kane's bid to become Governor* **far right** *is ruined by precisely the kind of scandal he printed in his own paper.*

impassioned radio appeal to America not to turn its head away but to get involved in the soon-to-be universal fight for freedom.

In the main, though, if such liberal sentiments found serious expression at all in the years 1940-1, they were firmly anchored in the past. No doubt it was still quite bold in 1940 to make a major film out of **The Grapes of Wrath**, John Steinbeck's grim novel of the Depression in rural America. The dustbowl years were, after all, not that far back – but with the full force of Darryl F. Zanuck's production facilities at 20th Century-Fox behind it, the poetic eye of John Ford guiding the camera and Henry Fonda leading an excellent cast, it was bound to be at least a formidable critical success. This quiet epic stirred audiences throughout the country while turning its back resolutely on anything that might be happening anywhere in the world other than America.

Darker visions

The two films of the period that would prove most important for the future of Hollywood movies, Orson Welles' **Citizen Kane** and John Huston's **The Maltese Falcon**, were equally oblivious of the outside world. And yet both films offered an index to the real tone of the times. Both were directorial debuts by Hollywood whiz-kids. Welles had been imported from the New York stage at the age of 26 with an unprecedented contract from RKO giving him a completely free hand to produce, write and direct his own films for his own unit. Huston, at 34, was already an experienced screenwriter who had worked on several major Warner Brothers films, including **Jezebel** (1938) and **High Sierra** (1941). And both films shared a darkness of viewpoint, a cool cynicism in their assessment of human nature, which became a vital factor in the Hollywood films of the late forties.

Citizen Kane was to have the most immediate effect. The story of a newspaper tycoon, based largely on the life of William Randolph Hearst and with Welles himself in the title role, it was put together like a jigsaw in a daringly fragmented structure. **Kane** put all Welles' ideas about cinema and life into the shop-window at once. Consequently it highlighted more technical innovations than any single film for decades, and other film-makers, even those who professed to despise Welles as an arty flash-in-the-pan, leapt with delight at the idea of deep-focus photography and low-angled shots. The former

served to keep foreground and background clearly visible at the same time, enabling elaborate and eloquent use of composition; the latter, a particular passion of Welles', enabled elements in the film frame to be emphasized (or diminished) in relation to their surroundings for a specific emotional effect.

It is unlikely that any of the technical "innovations" in the film were entirely new to movies, but the dash and vigor with which Welles used them, and his undoubted flair for publicity, made them seem so, and dramatized the art of film for moviegoers as never before. **Kane** had the reputation of being a financial disaster but, in fact, it wasn't. It had a longer shelf-life than most movies and soon recovered its negative cost. That did not make life any easier for the ambitious and temperamental Welles, and his subsequent films nearly all ran into financial difficulties and executive interference. But if there was a major Hollywood film to start the forties, it was undoubtedly the unforgettable film **Citizen Kane**.

In comparison, **The Maltese Falcon** looks at first sight like a modest and fairly conventional studio success – another private-eye thriller based on a Dashiell Hammett novel that had already been filmed twice before. But John Huston's film finally defined the very specific qualities of tough disenchantment (and possible soft center) that made Humphrey Bogart not only a star and a legend, but an icon for the decade. **The Maltese Falcon** lines up the duplicitous Brigid O'Shaughnessy (Mary Astor) against the gross Gutman (Sydney Greenstreet) and the effeminate Joel Cairo (Peter Lorre) in their search for the mysterious jewelled antique, and calls on private-eye Sam Spade (Bogart) to sort them out. Astor was the first of the forties breed of beautiful *femmes fatales*; Lorre and Greenstreet (aided by little Elisha Cook Jr in one of many small-fry gunmen roles he would play) were paired as unlikely partners-in-crime for the first time.

But, crucially, **The Maltese Falcon**, with its web of lies and deceit, its shadowy world of greed, ambiguity and murder, and above all the cynicism of Bogart, brought together many of the elements that would make up *film noir*. In other words, Huston flipped the cool, sophisticated *Thin Man* kind of thirties thriller straight into the dark and troubled world of the forties, creating a model for the kind of cruel, sceptical movie that was to dominate Hollywood later in the war after the first thrill of flag-waving patriotism had worn off.

Movie Mobilization 1942-3

Chapter 2

On 7 December 1941 the Japanese attacked the American naval base at Pearl Harbor and war was declared. At first there was a faint possibility that this conflict could be confined to the Pacific, but all such hopes were shattered when, four days later, Germany and Italy also declared war on the United States. The result in the film world was no more than a few seconds' stunned silence before the mad rush to be first on the new topical bandwagon of patriotic war movies began.

In the immediate pre-war period the American cinema had been going through an escapist phase, characterized best, perhaps, by **The Wizard of Oz** (1939) and **The Thief of Bagdad** (1940), both seen mainly in 1940. Even now, with hostilities declared, not everything became real, earnest and immediate. It might be said that many new films were styled to create a rose-tinted and far from realistic view of the war-torn world. A prime example of this was the Oscar-winning **Mrs Miniver** (1942), directed by William Wyler and starring Greer Garson in the title role of the plucky, resourceful, ever cheerful wife and mother withstanding the Blitz and Dunkirk and winning the war on the British home front. In general, however, there was a clear polarization between the films that one way or another took account of the war and films that clearly recognized an audience need for escapist entertainment in this time of strife.

First things first, of course. Poverty Row rushed into action immediately, and in no time at all Republic had managed to get on to American screens **Remember Pearl Harbor** (1942), so quickly and cheaply made that the attack itself had to take place off-screen, while the irresponsible American soldier hero was vainly struggling to get a message of warning to headquarters in time. He made up for this by achieving almost single-handed, and with optimistic speed, a victory in the Philippines.

Meanwhile the major studios, after a flurry of rapidly announced plans for topical war subjects, decided to hold off, as the speed of developments in the war quickly rendered many likely subjects outdated before they could even be made. Completion of Paramount's **Wake Island** (1942) for example, was held up for a few weeks in May 1942 awaiting the result of the military action in progress at that time – though the outcome proved to be less than cheering when it finally emerged. The main problem, in fact, for most of these immediate responses to the Pacific war was that they would have to dramatize defeat, since in the first four months of the war Japan was largely victorious. Therefore relatively realistic depictions such as **Bataan** (1943) had to stand on their heads to make a defeat

Right: *Defeat posing as moral victory in the East. In Tay Garnett's* **Bataan** *(1943), 13 American soldiers, including George Murphy (center left), Robert Taylor (center) and Lloyd Nolan (center right), are killed off one at a time by the ruthless Japanese.*

look like a victory, and only Paramount's **So Proudly We Hail** (1943) succeeded by being essentially a woman's picture in uniform.

Initially, Pacific war stories were difficult to depict as well as of doubtful appeal, and so studios started to pull back from their first premature enthusiasm. But the war in Europe was simpler to portray: lots of spies and secret service, suave and sinister Nazis and brave Europeans fighting them. In rapid succession moviegoers encountered French patriots in Jean Renoir's **This Land is Mine** (1943), with Charles Laughton, and **The Cross of Lorraine** (1943); an invaded Russian village in **North Star** (1943); Norwegian resistance in **The Moon is Down** and **Edge of Darkness** (both 1943); heroic Czechs in **Hitler's Madman** (1942) and the impressive **Hangmen Also Die!** (1943).

Few of these films had much distinction – Fritz Lang's **Hangmen Also Die!**, at least, was notable as the only Hollywood script by then resident Bertolt Brecht to reach the screen reasonably intact – but at least they provided starring roles for Paul Muni, Errol Flynn, Ann Sheridan, and even Gene Kelly, and proved quite popular for a while.

Right: *A beleaguered American unit holding on to a bridge at all costs in **Bataan** (1943). Although Bataan was a peninsula in the Philippines, near Manila, the film's plot much more closely resembles that of John Ford's **The Lost Patrol** (1934), set in the far-away Mesopotamian desert.*

Below: *Donald Barry (left) was more at home on the Western ranges of Republic serials and B movies than in the Philippines jungle of **Remember Pearl Harbor** (1942); but he was ably supported by Alan Curtis (right), now best remembered as the murder suspect desperately looking for an alibi in **Phantom Lady** (1944).*

Below: *Dr Franz Svoboda (Brian Donlevy) kills the top Nazi in Prague, Reinhard Heydrich, and escapes with the help of Mascha Novotny (Anna Lee) in Fritz Lang's **Hangmen Also Die!** (1943). Although the script was largely written by playwright Bertold Brecht, his role was played down and the screenplay was credited to John Wexley.*

You must remember this...

None of them were quite so popular, or for that matter quite so star-studded, as the model example of the genre, **Casablanca** (1943). Towards the end of her life Ingrid Bergman used to say that she had progressed from being delighted when anyone actually remembered **Casablanca** to being irritated that no one seemed to remember anything else. And it is true that the film's ascent to its present legendary status was quite gradual. But at the same time it is perfectly understandable, since all the elements come together with peculiar force and conviction.

The star power of the emotional triangle – Rick (Humphrey Bogart), Ilsa (Ingrid Bergman), Victor Laszlo (Paul Henreid) – is sufficient to keep audiences interested in the romance at the center of the story: will Ilsa make it up with Rick, with whom she previously had an affair and a misunderstanding, and stay with him, or will she do the noble thing and go away with her dedicated anti-Nazi husband? And with Conrad Veidt as the suave and supercilious Nazi Strasser, Claude Rains as the cynical but sympathetic Captain Renault, Dooley Wilson as Sam playing "As Time Goes By" and Peter Lorre and Sydney

Above: *Although timid French schoolmaster Albert Mory (Charles Laughton) is unable to declare his love for his colleague, Louise Martin (Maureen O'Hara), he takes the blame for her brother's Resistance activities and dies a hero in **This Land is Mine** (1943).*

Right: *Lovers Rick Blaine (Humphrey Bogart) and Ilsa Lund (Ingrid Bergman) sharing passion and champagne in pre-war Paris, before being parted by war, misunderstanding and her husband in **Casablanca** (1943), an evergreen classic of nostalgia.*

Greenstreet as disreputable inhabitants of Vichy North Africa, it is hardly surprising that after forty years the film still seems fresh.

The real secret of its success, then as now, is that its devisers, writer Howard Koch and director Michael Curtiz, knew uncannily well how to separate the topical issues of war, patriotism, honor and democracy, from the real concern — romance and the choices it involves. The fundamental things apply as time goes by...

Back home

Much safer, obviously, than frontline dispatches in fictional form or such romanticized or stiff-upper-lip tributes to the British home or society as **Mrs Miniver**, **Random Harvest** (1942), **Forever and a Day** (1943) and **The White Cliffs of Dover** (1944) were tributes to the American home. It was in **Since You Went Away** (1944) that Claudette Colbert provided America's answer to Mrs Miniver. She played a wife whose husband has been drafted, and she is left to defend the domestic fortress along with her two daughters, played by

Left: *Resistance leader Victor Laszlo (Paul Henreid), wife Ilsa and cafe owner Rick Blaine exchanging glances in the night in* **Casablanca**; *Sam (Dooley Wilson,* **above**) *is about to receive a request he just can't refuse; and Captain Renault (Claude Rains), collaborationist prefect of police* **top** *recruits Rick to help Laszlo and* Ilsa escape from the Nazis. After condoning the murder of a Gestapo captain, Renault's final act is to drop an empty bottle of Vichy water (symbol of the puppet French government based in that spa town) into a wastepaper basket. So the story's end is the beginning of "a beautiful friendship" between the two men.

Jennifer Jones and the teenage Shirley Temple, and with Hattie McDaniel as the black maid who is paid off in the interests of wartime economy. She also takes in a boarder (Charles Coburn), much as Jean Arthur had done in **The More the Merrier** (1943) to help combat a wartime accommodation shortage in Washington. About halfway through **Since You Went Away** a cable arrives to report the husband missing in action, but at the end another comes to say that he is all right and coming home. It is all too easy, at this distance in time, to make fun of such a confection, with its glossy unreality disguised as unsparing realism, but writer/producer David O. Selznick and director John Cromwell's film is still a persuasive vision of the American home "at war".

Such films did, after all, remind audiences of real problems in the real world at war. There were many other films being made in Hollywood at this time that took a quite opposite course, by turning their back completely on the war, and there were some, comedies and musicals especially, that aimed somewhere between the two. In **You'll Never Get Rich** (1941), Fred Astaire starts as a dance director sparring romantically with showgirl Rita Hayworth, and is then called up for military service and, by a series of convenient

Left: Anne Hilton (Claudette Colbert) receiving the wrong kind of cable giving news that her husband is missing in **Since You Went Away** (1944).

coincidences, is able to carry on both his career and his romance, while also achieving patriotic credit. But in the subsequent Astaire/Hayworth vehicle of the period, **You Were Never Lovelier** (1942) the war plays only an indirect role – the South American milieu of the story seems to be used mainly to show off Roosevelt's Good Neighbor policy towards Central and South America. Pan-American friendship was no doubt an important factor in a number of other, even lighter-weight movies of this time. Though it may seem to be forcing a point to analyze films starring Latin spitfires Carmen Miranda or Lupe Velez in political terms, undoubtedly they and the exotic settings of such films as **Down Argentine Way** (1940), **A Weekend in Havana** and **That Night in Rio** (both 1941) chimed so well with government policy that one wonders if they were entirely coincidental or the result of gentle persuasion.

Mobilizing the movies

A number of other films made before the United States actually entered the war played their part in preparing Americans to think of themselves again as a military nation. These include two of the biggest comedy hits of 1941, **Caught in the Draft**, a Bob Hope vehicle with a self-explanatory title, and **Buck Privates**, in which the newly popular comedy duo of Bud Abbott and Lou Costello were precipitated unwillingly into the Service. Here Bud and Lou go through all kinds of familiar slapstick situations and in the end emerge with a new respect for themselves, each other (they start out as spoilt heir and chauffeur but learn a lesson in democracy) and all the patriotic values of army and country. As the Andrews Sisters sing joyfully during the movie, "Red, white and blue/Are colors that look good on you".

Right above and below: *Bob Hope in **Caught in the Draft** (1941) in which he tries to avoid the draft but enlists by mistake — watched, **above**, by a none-too-impressed Dorothy Lamour.*

Below: *Rita Hayworth, as the aloof daughter of an Argentinian hotel owner, being swept off her feet by Fred Astaire, a New York dancer over-fond of the racetrack, in **You Were Never Lovelier** (1942). Although Hayworth's voice was dubbed over by singer Nan Wynn's for the "Dearly Beloved" number, she did all her own footwork in the dance routines. The film was enlivened by Jerome Kern's and Johnny Mercer's music and lyrics, and Xavier Cugat's Orchestra which added a Latin-American touch to the soundtrack.*

Left: *American Tim Baker (Tyrone Power) joins the British Royal Air Force and takes part in the heroic retreat from Dunkirk in Henry King's* **A Yank in the RAF** *(1941); he also wins the love of chorus girl Carol Brown (Betty Grable). King went on to make a more serious film of the life of American fliers in wartime England,* **Twelve O'Clock High** *(1949).*

Below: *Composer Irving Berlin (second from left) is among the rookies who "hate to get up in the morning" in the Warner Brothers extravaganza* **This Is the Army** *(1943), originally a Broadway hit put on for Army Emergency Relief. Ever-reliable Michael Curtiz directed.*

Another big hit of 1941 was **A Yank in the RAF**, in which American Tyrone Power joins the Royal Air Force at the time of the Battle of Britain, and though largely in pursuit of London showgirl Betty Grable, does along the way learn and project to audiences a high regard for the stiff-upper-lip British and their heroism in the defense of democracy. Robert Taylor and Errol Flynn both "joined the air force" for their studios in, respectively, **Flight Command** (1940) and **Dive Bomber** (1941), and many stars, male and female, had become familiar figures in uniform some time before Japan attacked Pearl Harbor.

Hollywood's first response to the war once it had become a reality was to take it more seriously than hitherto. Being drafted was suddenly no subject for comedy – but soon a natural desire for escape from the more worrying aspects of the conflict reasserted itself. With the need to maintain topicality in the face of a constantly changing military situation, this encouraged a certain slackening of intensity. There was more and more likelihood that the Forces would be celebrated in song and dance, in films liberally spiced with humor.

One of the biggest hits of 1943 was **This Is the Army**, a screen version of Irving Berlin's stage show for the troops which projected the comic interludes and easy, comfortable sentiment of army life – the kind where everyone hates to get up in the morning and ritual shirking and scrounging is not incompatible with a tear in the eye as one salutes the flag or thinks of lost comrades.

Paramount's **Star Spangled Rhythm** and Warner Brothers' **Thank Your Lucky Stars** (both 1943) had an even vaguer connection with wartime realities: the entertaining of a few suitably glamorized servicemen on leave was an excuse for all-star studio revues in which the house specialities were paraded or good-naturedly parodied. The atmosphere created by such films was deliberately informal – everyone pulling together for the war effort, whether by selling bonds, dancing with soldiers at the Hollywood Canteen, singing patriotic songs, or raising a laugh through the incongruity of Bette Davis growling about the men left at home, "They're Either Too Young or Too Old", or Paulette Goddard, Dorothy Lamour and Veronica Lake, reigning queens of Paramount, drawing humorous attention to their prime attributes in "A Sweater, a Sarong and a Peekaboo Bang".

There were, of course, even less direct expressions of American patriotism and solidarity with the war effort; a film like Warners' biography of George M. Cohan, **Yankee Doodle Dandy** (1942), being a celebration of a major show-business personality with a role tailor-made for James Cagney, might in principle have been made at any time, but in 1942 it gave more emphasis to the patriotism of the great Broadway man who wrote "Over There" and was quite shameless about hitting audiences over the head with its jingoistic message.

Such films counted as "serious"; Cagney even got an Oscar for his impersonation of Cohan. Sentimentality was definitely in, but audiences could not stomach ruthless or satirical approaches to the war. Ernst Lubitsch's **To Be or Not to Be** (1942) was a prime example. A

comedy about Polish actors caught up in the invasion of their country, it expressly makes the point that actors are actors first, and political beings way afterwards. Legend has it that at the main preview everything went smoothly until it got to the line, delivered by Sig Ruman as an idiotic Gestapo officer, in which Jack Benny's Hamlet is commented on, thus: "Believe me, what he did to Shakespeare we are now doing to Poland." From this point, witnesses insist, laughter died and the film was castigated as, at best, unfeeling and in bad taste, at worst a vicious attempt by the "Berlin-born" (though Jewish) Lubitsch to play Goebbels's game and support the Nazi cause.

Lubitsch and his co-producer, the Hungarian-born British film mogul Alexander Korda, were left mystified: did a war mean that all sense of humor had to go by the board, that the eccentricities of one's allies could not be the occasion of a little teasing? The answer, for the moment, was a resounding "yes".

Left and right: *The ebullient George M. Cohan (James Cagney) is riding high in* **Yankee Doodle Dandy** *(1942), one of several showbiz pictures directed by the indefatigable Michael Curtiz, who (according to Peter Ustinov) had a long career in Hollywood despite the handicap that he "forgot his native Hungarian without taking the precaution of learning any other language".*

Cagney, who started as a song-and-dance man, won an Oscar for his Portrayal of Cohan. Orson Welles has said of him that his performances are "always unreal and always true".

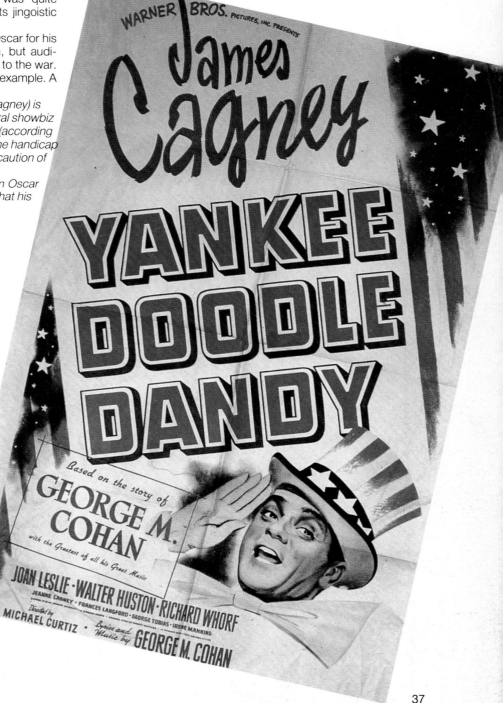

Disney's war

But what was Hollywood doing when it was not concerning itself in any appreciable way with the war? Certainly at the forefront of escapist cinema in the dark days of 1942-3 were Walt Disney's films. Though the Disney animation studio did its bit for the war effort with directly instructional films like **Victory Through Air Power** (1943) and tactful tributes to the Good Neighbor policy like **Saludos Amigos** (1943) and **The Three Caballeros** (1945), its central concern was still magical entertainment for the whole family, whether with a self-consciously cultural slant – as in **Fantasia**, which

Left and below: *Fantasia* (1940; general release by RKO, 1942) put animated pictures to a series of popular orchestral pieces, played by the Philadelphia Orchestra, conducted by Leopold Stokowski. One of adviser Deems Taylor's more adventurous choices was Stravinsky's "The Rite of Spring" (1913), originally composed as a ballet score for Diaghilev's company. Its dissonances and jagged rhythms suggested to the Disney team the creation and evolution of a savage world in which dinosaurs struggle for survival and destroy each other in a process of Darwinian selection.

"The Concert Feature" section originated with the idea of starring Mickey Mouse in a short feature, backed by music from "The Sorcerer's Apprentice" (1897) by Dukas. This finally became one of the most popular sections of the completed film, now endlessly reshown on television.

Mickey is a trainee magician who knows how to start a spell to help him with the household chores but cannot control it. He is quickly overwhelmed by multiplying brooms (eventually 16 of them) and cascading buckets of water.

Pinocchio (1940) carried to new heights the experiments with the multi-plane Technicolor begun in **Fantasia.** But the process was too elaborate and expensive, so that **Pinocchio** remains technically supreme and unique among Disney's creations. Based on Carlo Collodi's story, it describes how a boy puppet is made by the old puppet-maker Geppetto, who longs for a son **left**. Brought to life by the Blue Fairy (below) to the accompaniment of "When You Wish Upon a Star", Pinocchio soon begins to be confusedly aware of human desires and temptations **bottom**, later symbolized by a monstrous nose and then by even more grotesque attributes.

Left and below left: *Pinocchio*'s conscience is Jiminy Cricket, given a marvellously moralistic voice by Cliff Edwards (Pinocchio's voice was Dickie Jones). Other new friends are Figaro the cat and Cleo the confident goldfish.

Below: In *Dumbo* (1941) a baby elephant with giant ears is given a flying lesson by some at first not very friendly crows – who sing disbelievingly, "When I See an Elephant Fly", to the much-mocked infant pachyderm.

Bottom: *Bambi* (1942) relates the adventures of a young fawn and his forest friends, such as Thumper the rabbit and Flower the skunk. But the real star of the film is the beautifully animated forest itself.

illustrated a whole program of classical music in easily comprehensible terms – or the fairy-tale approach of **Pinocchio** (1940), **Dumbo** (1941) and **Bambi** (1942).

It was surely an important part of these films' appeal that nothing could be further removed from the reality of war. And in this heyday of the animated feature there was even room for others, notably Max Fleischer's **Gulliver's Travels** (1939) and his parable of insects heading for a rooftop paradise, **Mr Bug Goes to Town** (1941).

Babes in Hollywood

Meanwhile the musicals of the early forties willingly emphasized those elements that removed them from real life. They might be set in an MGM never-never land of wholesome teenagers perpetually putting on a show; from **Babes in Arms** (1939) to **Babes on Broadway** (1941), Judy Garland and Mickey Rooney seldom seemed to do anything else.

At 20th Century-Fox their leading ladies – Betty Grable, Alice Faye, Carmen Miranda, Sonja Henie – appeared in a number of unlikely locations, entirely re-created on the studio backlot, in which Rio and Havana were virtually indistinguishable from the Rockies in springtime or Miami with a moon over it. In their films there was never more than a whiff of war. At most one of the male characters might be drafted, so that his beloved could dream musically of him or comical

Below: *Cabin in the Sky* (1943), the first all-black musical since *Hallelujah!* (1929), was also Vincente Minnelli's directorial debut. The hero, played by radio star Eddie "Rochester" Anderson, is torn between his virtuous wife (Ethel Waters) and the enticing Georgia Brown (Lena Horne). Here Georgia takes time off from seduction while "Shine" is performed by Willie Best (at piano) and the talented singer/dancer John W. "Bubbles" Bublett.

Below right: *Babes in Arms* (1939), directed by ex-Warners choreographer Busby Berkeley for MGM, was the original "kids putting on a show" musical. The "show" featured two blackface numbers, "The Darktown Strutters' Ball" and "My Daddy Was a Minstrel Man". Here Mickey Rooney (left) is being upstaged by the "white" star, Douglas McPhail, with Betty Jaynes. His regular co-star in MGM musicals, Judy Garland, is offstage in this scene.

misunderstandings could arise when he came home on furlough. The classic example of all this is **The Gang's All Here** (1943), a Busby Berkeley extravaganza that permits Alice Faye to sing one of the key songs of the war years, "No Love, No Nothing (Until My Baby Comes Home)", while her soldier-hero extricates himself from a romance with someone else. Also here the "Lady in the Tutti-Frutti Hat" number was the apotheosis of Carmen Miranda's career, and the film climaxes with one of those surrealistic Berkeley numbers that had made him the greatest dance director of the thirties, when the innocent-sounding "Polka-Dot Polka" turns into a bizarre fantasy and the grand finale merges into "A Journey to a Star" with all the mad imagery that implies. The whole intention of this dazzlingly achieved movie was to make its audience forget the war and enter the magic world that was created by Hollywood alone.

Heaven's gate?

There were other types of screen fantasies being made at this time. In **Cabin in the Sky** (1943), for instance, Vincente Minnelli, an important directorial recruit from the Broadway stage, created a beguiling all-black heaven and hell, with angels and devils fighting musically for the souls of mortals. Heavenly (or hellish) intervention in human affairs was, in fact, very popular in early forties films. Entries include William Dieterle's stylish period piece **All That Money Can Buy**, Alexander Hall's **Here Comes Mr Jordan** (both 1941), and Lubitsch's **Heaven Can Wait** (1943). Lubitsch's contribution to the cycle is probably the best – it features a great performance from suave Don Ameche as the average man given a chance to look over the faults of his life and, if he can, make amends. This film saw probably the last flourish of the famed "Lubitsch touch", especially in its visual depiction of the geography of hell. Yet another piece of

supernatural hokum was René Clair's **I Married a Witch** (1942), starring Veronica Lake as a Salem witch returning from the dead to fall in love with one of her persecutor's descendants (Fredric March).

These films took a fairly sunny view of the supernatural. But there was little or no actual magic in the series of vaguely Arabian Nights entertainments that poured out of Universal in the wake of Korda's **The Thief of Bagdad** (1940). In such films as **Arabian Nights** (1942) and **White Savage** (1943) the atmosphere remained happily fantastical – perhaps because it was difficult to take the resident temptress Maria Montez, with her heavy Latin accent and impassive acting style, too seriously in anything. Probably the best of these films, which also starred muscular Jon Hall and Turkish Turhan Bey, was **Ali Baba and the Forty Thieves** (1943), co-starring Sabu. However, the genre retained its slightly tatty charms through many variations like **Gypsy Wildcat** (1944), which updated the fantasy to an eighteenth century setting; **Sudan** (1945), with Bey as a slave prince; and, perhaps best and most bizarre of all, Robert Siodmak's **Cobra Woman** (1944), in which Jon Hall was a modern mariner wrecked on a forgotten Pacific paradise ruled by evil Maria Montez – ever busy sending all the available women up to bathe fatally in the "fire of eternal life" while her good twin waits in the wings wringing her hands until the inevitable volcanic eruption ends it all.

Above: *Double value for fans of Maria Montez in* **Cobra Woman** *(1944). She plays two parts – an evil South Seas priestess who is obsessed by snakes, and her virtuous sister. Here she is the cobra woman, with Lon Chaney Jr and Indian boy Sabu.*
Right: *The famous staircase quarrel, from* **The Magnificent Ambersons** *(1942), between spoiled George Amberson Minafter (Tim Holt) and his hysterical maiden Aunt Fanny (Agnes Moorehead).*

After Kane

Not all reflections on the supernatural were quite so cheerful, and it was at RKO that an horrific new trend grew up in the early forties. Before we look at Val Lewton's macabre movies, however, another, non-supernatural, masterpiece from RKO must be considered. This is 1942's **The Magnificent Ambersons**, a grim story of family decline with some of the most exquisite, sensitive and penetrating film-making ever done by Orson Welles, whose follow-up to **Citizen Kane** this was. It contained nothing even peripherally connected with the war; sadly, it was tampered with, though not made more popular, while Welles was away in South America making a tribute to the Good Neighbor policy, the unfinished **It's All True**, at the direct instigation of Washington.

But the most influential RKO film at this time was far less costly and prestigious than the beautiful **Ambersons**. It was a zero-budget horror film called **Cat People** (1942), made by Lewton, who was a new graduate to production. It gave a first chance at directing to Welles' editor, Robert Wise, and chose (largely of economic necessity) to create its effects by absence, darkness, suggestion, recognizing that the horror our own minds can create, stalking undefined in the shadows, is bound to be infinitely more frightening than any extra in an ill-fitting cat-suit. The film was one of the great "sleepers" of its time, achieving such unexpected success that it led to a succession of Lewton productions in the same mould – **I Walked With a Zombie**, **The Seventh Victim**, **Leopard Man** (all 1943) and **Curse of the Cat People** (1944).

The popularity of the Lewton cycle can be attributed to audiences looking for distraction from the very real menace outside by seeking out psychologically manageable horrors. It was a good trick as long as it could be pulled off. But by 1944 the lurker in the shadows was less a supernatural cat than a very contemporary con man, killer or broad on the make. It was the time of *film noir*, that most characteristic of wartime Hollywood genres, and neurosis could no longer be confined to an alternative world, a nightmare that would evaporate as soon as one ceased to suspend one's disbelief.

Left: *Alice Moore (Jane Randolph) in* **Cat People** *(1942), moments after having bumped into a clawed creature in the swimming pool. Here she shows her ripped robe to Blondie (Mary Halsey).*

Below: *"Can you tell me how to get to . . . ?" Jessica Holland (Christine Gordon) and friend Betsy (Frances Dee) being stopped on the way to the local voodoo ceremony in* **I Walked With a Zombie** *(1943).*

Escape to the Shadows 1944-5

Chapter 3

John Cromwell's film **Since You Went Away**, that hymn to the American home in 1943, did not come out until 1944, and by then it was strangely anachronistic. Most of the married American men who were going off to war had already gone – including such movie stars as Henry Fonda, James Stewart, Robert Taylor and the recently widowed Clark Gable (his wife, the star Carole Lombard, had been killed in a plane crash while on tour selling war bonds) – and the women they left behind had got used to it.

Since You Went Away was indeed made with the idea of enshrining the recent past rather than reflecting the immediate present. But, oddly enough, it was out of touch in its psychological rather than its physical presentation: it offered up a sanitized world where all worries could be dealt with by good will and fortitude; the war, though troublesome and painful for many, was still kept safely in an airtight compartment, somewhere over there. But by 1944 neither film-makers nor audiences saw it quite that way anymore.

It was not that the war in the Pacific and in Europe had moved centerscreen either, for most of the dark Hollywood dramas and thrillers that dominated the period do not specify very clearly when they are taking place, though generally it is in a world that is clearly not at war. In that respect, at least, *film noir* – a term later coined for the movement by appreciative French critics – could be regarded as escapist. But these films cannot be explained so easily as the Val Lewton horror cycle of the mid forties and its offshoots, for example. This time the horror is interior, something you cannot run away from.

Black souls

Superficially, "horror" might seem an overstatement of what *film noir* actually presented. Certainly some of the classics of the genre, such as **Gaslight** or **The Lodger** (both 1944), are on the verge of the psychological horror movie. But **Laura** (1944), the film that more than any other started it all off, is not a horror film, nor are **Phantom Lady, The Woman in the Window, Double Indemnity** (all 1944) or **Mildred Pierce** (1945), to cite a handful of the more obvious examples. They definitely open up a dark world of powerful and perverse passions for us, but that is not quite the same thing, and not so easy to shrug off. The "black" of *film noir* is literally the blackness of night and metaphorically the blackness of the soul of at least one major character.

Fear, greed and lust for power are at the root of much of the *film noir*'s action, and insanity or obsession frequently provides the paradoxical rationale. The locale is usually Los Angeles or some other

Right: *In George Cukor's splendid version of* **Gaslight** *(1944), sadistic Gregory Anton (Charles Boyer) tries to drive his wife Paula (Ingrid Bergman) mad while unearthing the family jewels. She gains her revenge after he's caught – she pretends that she really is mad and capable of anything . . .*

unnamed American urban hell, but it may be somewhere slightly offbeat, at a period somewhat removed in time – **The Lodger**'s London in the nineties, say, or the American West of **Pursued** (1947) – but the links with everyday life must remain strong.

An American nightmare

It has been usual to credit the group of German and Austrian emigrés who came to prominence in Hollywood at this time for the appearance of *film noir*, and to link it with the *Angst*-ridden German Expressionist cinema of the silent era. But that is a drastic over-simplification. It is true that **Laura**, normally regarded as the first fully fledged Hollywood *film noir*, was directed by the Viennese Otto Preminger after the first director, Rouben Mamoulian, had been fired,

but the origins of the project and its materials were entirely American.

Robert Siodmak, the director of **Phantom Lady**, a small-budget surprise success, was born in Memphis but raised in Leipzig and had become a notable film-maker in Germany, but worked in the opposite camp to Expressionism. His **Menschen am Sonntag** (1929), co-directed by a genuine maker of Gothic horror films, Edgar G. Ulmer, and with the assistance of the young Billy Wilder and Fred Zinnemann, was a working-class comedy that pioneered location realism. Wilder himself was primarily known as a writer and director of comedy when he made **Double Indemnity**, and the *film noir* genre was well established in Hollywood before Fritz Lang, a more convincing example of an Expressionist director, turned to it with **The Woman in the Window** and **Scarlet Street** (1945).

Left: *Jack the Ripper (Laird Cregar) is about to find another victim in* **The Lodger** *(1944). The movie was a remake of Alfred Hitchcock's 1926 film by John Brahm, who appropriately began his film career in London.*

Above: *In* **Laura** *(1944), a decadent columnist (Clifton Webb), a self-indulgent playboy (Vincent Price), his ex-mistress (Judith Anderson), an obsessed detective (Dana Andrews) – and a portrait of Laura (Gene Tierney) provide a complex network of jealousy and murder.*

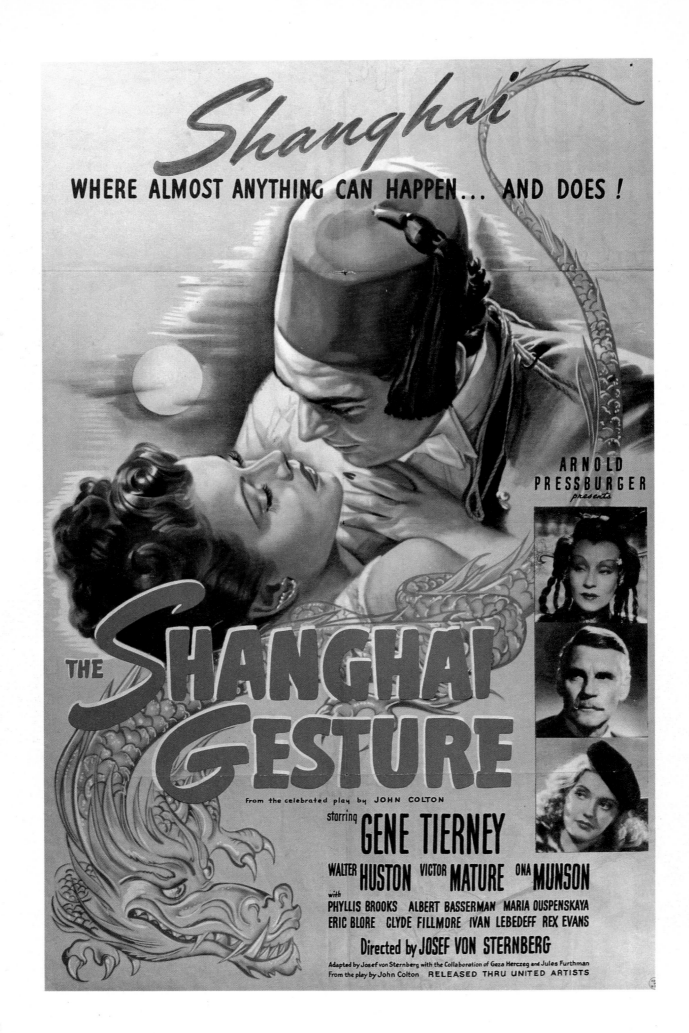

Before night fell...

In any case, the audiences to whom these dark dramas proved so instantly attractive were almost entirely American. If we suppose that the European emigrés had some kind of intuitive knowledge of how to cater to the taste for such a dark world, the presence and nature of the need has still to be explained. Earlier in the forties there had been one or two films that anticipated *film noir*. In 1941 Josef von Sternberg came up with his last bizarre masterpiece, an opulent version of the old stage shocker **The Shanghai Gesture**. Its brothel location was not exactly emphasized, but the film is still full of perfumed perversity and the kind of twisted eroticism that became crucial to the new form.

In 1943 Alfred Hitchcock made his first truly American film, **Shadow of a Doubt**, about the going into hiding of a murderer (Joseph Cotten) with his small-town family and his final exposure, at least in the eyes of his doting niece (Teresa Wright). Though the film was noted at the time for its innovatory use of real locations (in the West Coast town of Santa Rosa), and most of the menace lies hidden under the implacable glare of the Californian sun, the plot material, the suggestions of decay, and the heroine's almost fatal brush with evil and obsession, at once link it with the *film noir* proper of only a year or so later. Although Sternberg was another Viennese and Hitchcock a Londoner, these were clearly *Hollywood* films, as were the pivotal works in *film noir*'s studio origins, **Citizen Kane** and **The Maltese Falcon** (both 1941).

Left: *The Shanghai Gesture* (1941) was Josef von Sternberg's only feature movie of the forties, an unrestrained fantasy of oriental decadence set in a gambling den where chance and destiny conspire to destroy doomed, unhappy lives.

Above: *The Shanghai Gesture* is a monument to the doomed. Mother Gin-Sling (Ona Munson) controls the wretched lives of the gamblers who patronize her establishment, hiding all emotions behind a masklike countenance. Her vulnerable, drug-addicted Eurasian daughter Poppy is played by Gene Tierney.
Below: In Alfred Hitchcock's **Shadow of a Doubt** (1943), Uncle Charlie (Joseph Cotten), the "Merry Widow" murderer, seeks refuge in a small Californian town. Unluckily for him he's front page news, and his attempts to remove the story in front of his niece while pretending that he's performing a trick only increase her suspicions.

54

Left: *"A tragic and eternal work of art"* was how critic James Agee described William Wellman's **The Story of GI Joe** (1945). It was based on the reminiscences of Pulitzer Prize-winning war correspondent Ernie Pyle (Burgess Meredith, center), who goes through the Italian campaign with Captain Walker (Robert Mitchum, left) and his men, sharing their hazards and mourning their losses. The film ends with the death of Walker in an attack on a monastery near Rome. The real-life Ernie Pyle later went to the Pacific front where (like many of the soldier actors) he was killed in action.

Below: *Also about the Italian campaign, Lewis Milestone's* **A Walk in the Sun** *(1945) concentrated on a single morning during the Salerno landings, south of Naples, in 1943 and the attempt of an American battalion to capture a German emplacement.*
Dana Andrews is the sergeant (front left) conferring with John Ireland (center) and Lloyd Bridges (front right). The fatalistic screenplay, from Harry Brown's novel, was by Robert Rossen, who went on to direct **Body and Soul** *(1947),* **All the King's Men** *(1949) and, much later,* **The Hustler** *(1961).*

Dark corners

When the fully conceived *film noir* arrived on the scene, it arrived with a vengeance. Suddenly, in 1944 it seemed that every film in sight had dramatic low-key lighting, was full of mysterious pursuits through rainwashed streets and otherwise took place in small basement bars or overstuffed "artistic" apartments. No situation depicted was without its *femme fatale*, its secretly demented artist, its effete and sexually obsessed wit, its murder and mayhem as a part of normal expectation, and its innocents, male and female, caught in the toils of a strange life they cannot understand. And sometimes the innocent are as doomed as the guilty – perhaps more so, since they lack the perception to defend themselves. It was, indeed, a depressing landscape that was under scrutiny at this less than cheering point in world history. It was even odder still, perhaps, since the prospect of Allied defeat in the war had faded and been replaced by a rapid and fairly confident victory following the opening of a Western front in Europe on 6 June 1944.

The road to glory?

We can only speculate why a taste for picturesque gloom and studies of the trapped, helpless and hopeless should have dominated American cinema at this time of outward advance and hope. A key to it might be provided if we look at the war and the films that depicted it. During the three-and-a-half years America was directly involved in World War II precisely this happened: the heroic expectations of the American public and the American cinema in 1942-3 had gradually worn out, to be replaced by an anti-heroic view of war as a painful necessity with precious little glory. A characteristic war film of the period was William Wellman's **The Story of GI Joe** (1945). Here, war correspondent Ernie Pyle (portrayed by Burgess Meredith in the film), who wrote the source book **Here Is the War**, insisted in his contract that there should be no extraneous heroics, and the picture was accordingly gritty, downbeat and sympathetic to the plight of the wretched soldiers.

Lewis Milestone contributed **The Purple Heart** (1944), in which a group of captured American flyers are tortured by the Japanese with no eventual reprieve (despite some appalling jingoism), and **A Walk in the Sun** (1945), a similarly fatalistic picture of the slow grind of war and the virtual inevitability of death for the majority. None of this could be described as outright pacifism, but these films generally eschewed war glory in favor of one which saw the dreadful conflict as an unwanted necessity.

Trouble on the home front

In the circumstances, it is not surprising that the "civilian" cinema should have been so preoccupied with neurosis. Frequently, though not always, *film noir*'s nasty goings-on involve the privileged classes: old money tries to protect itself in any imaginable way, artists and intellectuals hide murderous frenzy behind a suave and debonair façade, the family has endless horrors committed in its name. That pattern is applied to most of the famous firsts of the genre.

In **Phantom Lady** the fundamentally decent characters are entangled in a dark, night-time world of madness, represented by the opposite poles of the cool artist killer and the lady in the hat, the only person who could establish the hero's innocence of his wife's murder if she had not gone irrevocably mad from the pangs of love. In **Laura** virtually everybody around the mysterious vanished figure of Laura herself (Gene Tierney) is vicious and corrupt, peddling flesh or harboring obsessive jealousy and possessiveness behind a mask of cynical wit; Clifton Webb here played one of *film noir*'s most compelling villains in the acid Waldo Lydekker. In **Christmas Holiday** (1944) nice Deanna Durbin marries charming New Orleans playboy Gene Kelly only to find that he is a gambler, an embezzler and ultimately a murderer, aided and abetted by his classy mother, with whom he is linked in suspicious closeness. In **Dark Waters** (1944), rich but vulnerable Merle Oberon is almost driven mad by evil supposed friends and relatives after her property. In **Gaslight** rich Ingrid Bergman is driven almost mad by avaricious husband Charles Boyer, searching for an inheritance she does not even know she has.

The suffocating nineties setting of **Gaslight** recurs also in **Hangover Square** (1944), a curious but brilliantly atmospheric reworking of another Patrick Hamilton work, which transfers it from the uneasy Munich atmosphere of 1938 to a Victorian world where the composer hero undergoes a Jekyll-and-Hyde transformation (supposedly schizophrenic) to become a sex murderer by night. The same idea of the artist/intellectual as unbalanced and potentially evil had occurred in the 1941 version of **Dr Jekyll and Mr Hyde** itself, with Spencer Tracy as the schizophrenic hero flaying Ingrid Bergman and Lana Turner. And the theme was repeated in Albert Lewin's culture-littered **The Picture of Dorian Gray** (1945), starring Hurd Hatfield. Meanwhile, John Brahm, who had directed Laird Cregar in **Hangover Square**, made **The Lodger**, a fictionalization of Jack the Ripper, also starring Cregar.

Left: Brian Cameron (Joseph Cotten) in **Gaslight** (1944) plays the Scotland Yard detective who is falling in love with Paula Anton (Ingrid Bergman), sharing her suspicions that husband Gregory (played by Charles Boyer) is trying to drive her mad. Bergman won an Oscar and Boyer was nominated; more remarkably, seventeen-year-old Angela Lansbury, a refugee from the London blitz, was nominated for the best supporting actress award in her first role — a cockney maid.

Above: John Brahm's second — and last — good film was **Hangover Square** (1945), based on the novel by Patrick Hamilton. The cast seemed to have been cursed. Laird Cregar (left) slimmed so drastically for his part as a demented pianist-composer who murders beautiful women that he died, aged just 28. Linda Darnell seen here as a typically sluttish femme fatale, survived for another twenty years but was burned to death in a house fire in Chicago.

A touch of Germanic dread

All of these films, amazingly, emerged in 1944-5. But they do not exhaust the list. There are *films noirs*, also, that take place in much more basic suburban society or take their characters down to depths of social and sexual degradation all the more alarming because they do not have, like **The Lodger**, the saving and distancing grace of period picturesqueness. No doubt the greatest degradation suffered by any "hero" at this time was that meted out to Edward G. Robinson in Fritz Lang's **The Woman in the Window** and **Scarlet Street**.

In his native Germany Lang had accustomed himself to the fact that the world was a dark and dangerous place in **Dr Mabuse der Spieler** (1922) and other early films, and there are, of course, great moments of bleakness in his **Die Nibelungen** saga of 1924 and futuristic epic **Metropolis** (1927). But it is **M** (1931), in which Peter Lorre plays a child-murderer, that most powerfully foreshadows the tortured, guilty passions of Lang's *noir* period in Hollywood. Arriving in America in 1934, Lang took time to learn about American society before delivering such caustic comments on it as **Fury** (1936) and **You Only Live Once** (1937). His Edward G. Robinson/Joan Bennett films then perfectly caught the mood of the times.

Left: *Complications set in in Otto Preminger's **Fallen Angel** (1945). Stella the waitress is nothing but trouble for her admirer Eric Stanton (center), who decides to marry Alice Faye for her money. With this, he hopes to pacify and win over Stella. Alas, on his wedding night longed-for Stella is murdered by another lover, who then sets about finding Eric to add to his kill. As luck would have it, Eric chose well in Alice Faye who shields him from the worst and proves her love, enabling the film to resolve itself happily for audience and participants alike.*

Above: ***The Woman in the Window** (1944). Professor Richard Wanley (Edward G. Robinson) admires a portrait of Alice Reed (Joan Bennett) in a store window, but soon regrets meeting its original subject, who ensnares him in a nightmare of murder and blackmail.*

In **The Woman in the Window** Robinson plays a mild and innocent professor who gets entangled with a beautiful but dangerous kept woman and so inevitably with blackmail and murder. In **Scarlet Street** he is a timid clerk who is also a gifted Sunday painter, held hopelessly in thrall by trashy Joan Bennett even to the extent of letting her pass off his paintings as hers while she kicks him around and insults him; in one classic sado-masochistic moment she makes him varnish her toenails with the laconic order, "Here. You're a painter. Paint these."

Otto Preminger's **Fallen Angel** (1945) dissects small-town life with admirable irony: a man marries for money (but not very much) just so that he can keep his place in the affections of the town slut, desired by all. If this was small-time duplicity, **Double Indemnity** was big-time. Here, Barbara Stanwyck's evil wife, with her eyes set on adultery and her husband's insurance, and with her vulgar blonde bangs and suggestive ankle-bracelet, is one of the definitive *femmes fatales* of the forties. She easily seduces the compliant insurance agent, played by Fred MacMurray, into helping her murder her husband for his money, and the intrigue this pair is involved in, set in shuttered Spanish-Colonial rooms, and bleak, anonymous supermarkets, is unforgettably sour and unappetizing.

In one sense all these films are escapist: they not only avoid almost all mention of the war, even though the setting of most of them is clearly contemporary, but they also reach areas of life – and death – that must have been far from the everyday concerns of the average audience. For example, they probed the still "exotic" worlds of psychiatry and psychoanalysis, which became fashionable in films like Hitchcock's **Spellbound** (1945), where Ingrid Bergman resolves Gregory Peck's amnesia with the help of a dream sequence by Salvador Dali; William Dieterle's **Love Letters** (1945), where Joseph

Below and left: *In Alfred Hitchcock's **Spellbound** (1945) Dr Constance Peterson (Ingrid Bergman) is in for a shock as she discovers that the new head of the clinic where she works, "Dr Edwardes" (Gregory Peck), is an impostor. He is really John Ballantine, suffering loss of memory and under the illusion that he may have murdered the real Edwardes. But with the help of her trusty old psychiatry professor (played by Michael Chekhov, the playwright's nephew) she establishes her lover's innocence and exposes the real killer.*

Cotten resolves Jennifer Jones' trauma over the death of her first husband; and Billy Wilder's **The Lost Weekend** (1945), where Jane Wyman works valiantly to retrieve Ray Milland from alcoholism on the assumption that explaining his weakness – a writer's block – will explain it away. In America at the time few filmgoers would have been personally acquainted with a psychiatrist, or knew more about psychiatry than might be gleaned from *Readers' Digest*; these films offered fresh insights.

Mother's ruin

Only one of the really important *films noirs* of the period touched on the real lives of those in the audience, or at least on their dreams, ambitions and fears. This was **Mildred Pierce**, based on a novel by James M. Cain, which returned Joan Crawford to major stardom after some years in the doldrums. The film is a very interesting combination of old and new elements. In many of her thirties films at MGM Crawford had played a character clawing her way up the social

Far left: *Joan Crawford is in for a rough time in and as* **Mildred Pierce** *(1945). She plays a successful business woman who unwisely takes up with wealthy playboy Monty Berrigan (Zachary Scott), marries him, and finds herself under police suspicion when he is murdered.*

Below: *Ray Milland as alcoholic Don Birnam in Billy Wilder's* **The Lost Weekend** *(1945). Critic James Agee commented: ''I undershtand that liquor interesh: innerish: intereshtsh are rather worried about thish film. Thash tough.''*

and financial ladder, to represent a version of the basic American success story – though there was almost always a message suggesting material success could not itself bring happiness.

Crawford as Mildred Pierce bakes pies to become a restaurant tycoon, all for the sake of her daughter, who grows up into a spoiled and snobbish little minx ready to reject her mother for her "commonness" and steal her mother's man in the bargain. She also kills him and expects mother to take the blame. Michael Curtiz's direction presents a mixture of *film noir* fatalism, successful careerism, the decadence of the rich and idle, and the psychological implications of obsessive mother-love. No wonder the film, aided by

the moody, low-key art direction of Anton Grot and photography of Ernest Haller, was a runaway success that launched a whole series of pictures in which Crawford suffered in the greatest luxury, a revolver tucked away in the pocket of every mink.

Down these mean streets

Another trend was indicated by **Double Indemnity**, in that it was based on a James M. Cain story and scripted by the most distinguished practitioner of that particular kind of disenchanted American thriller novel, Raymond Chandler. Several of Chandler's own novels were to find their way onto the screen in the next two or

Love trouble in **Double Indemnity** (1944). Insurance investigator Barton Keyes (Edward G. Robinson, **left**) reluctantly comes to realize that his younger colleague, salesman Walter Neff, is involved with scheming Phyllis Dietrichson **below** in a plot to kill her husband and collect the insurance money. However, the murderous duo soon come to distrust each other, which – in a typical James M. Cain finale – leads to their violent end. Cain's story is supposed to have been based on the notorious Ruth Snyder case of 1927.

three years, starting with **Murder, My Sweet** in 1945, and followed by **The Big Sleep, The Brasher Doubloon** and **The Blue Dahlia** (a screen original) in 1946, and **The Lady in the Lake** in 1947. In 1946 Cain's most famous book, **The Postman Always Rings Twice**, was also filmed for the first time in America (it had already been filmed without authorization in France and Italy).

These films make a coherent group because they all share a certain sour romanticism and a bleak California location. Both Cain and Chandler claim to be tough and disillusioned, but in fact they both hide a soft, idealistic center beneath the deadpan cynicism. Chandler in particular tends to make of his private eye Philip Marlowe a sort of contemporary knight on a quest for lost innocence. The character, variously embodied by Dick Powell (**Murder, My Sweet**), George Montgomery (**The Brasher Doubloon**), Robert Montgomery (virtually unseen in the subjective camerawork of **The Lady in the Lake**) and, magisterially, by Humphrey Bogart (**The Big Sleep**), always retains the heroic lineaments beyond the outwardly gruff and spiky exterior.

Bogart was the greatest Marlowe, perhaps because he was like him in real life. Certainly man and myth have now become one in the popular imagination. Emerging out of the shadows of the war and *film noir*, Bogart became the greatest cinematic icon of the period because his Marlowe, his Sam Spade and his Rick in **Casablanca** were each, in Chandler's words, a man "who is not himself mean, who is neither tarnished nor afraid", for all that he has been bruised by experience. The Bogart hero, pug-ugly, rasping, trench-coated and smoking, caught exactly that forties mood of disenchantment but never bowed to sentiment or cruelty. Beginning with hoodlums in the mid thirties, Bogart had gone on to more complex gangsters in films like **High Sierra** (1941), and by the time of **The Maltese Falcon** was a major star. If we remember him best as Rick, it is his two films for

Left: Raymond Chandler's only screen original, **The Blue Dahlia** (1946), is a too predictable tale of a war veteran (Alan Ladd) whose unfaithful wife is murdered by his unstable best friend. He is suspected, but fortunately a young blonde passer-by (Veronica Lake) helps him to prove his innocence.

Above: Private-eye Philip Marlowe (Humphrey Bogart) prepares to defend himself against vicious gambler Eddie Mars and his thugs, ably supported by wealthy client Vivian Rutledge (Lauren Bacall) in **The Big Sleep** (1946). This was easily the best Chandler adaptation before Robert Altman's **The Long Goodbye** (1973).

Below and right: *The Postman Always Rings Twice* (1946) was based on James Cain's 1934 novel of murder, jealousy and betrayal set in the small towns and suburbs of Southern California. Cora Smith (Lana Turner), bored by her elderly, kindly husband and his lonely roadside café develops a taste for excitement at the sight of handsome drifter Frank Chambers who happens by and decides to stay on as handyman.

Howard Hawks, **The Big Sleep** and **To Have and Have Not** (1945), that brought him his finest moments, as well as Lauren Bacall.

When Bogart is Marlowe we are left in no doubt that the streets he traverses are very mean indeed, while the occasional brushes with riches – as in his employer's household in **The Big Sleep** – show something as decadent and corrupt as one could imagine, at any rate within the bounds of the Production Code at that time.

The Code was circumvented another way in Tay Garnett's simmering version of **The Postman Always Rings Twice**. Despite the much-vaunted freedom that permitted a sexually explicit version with Jack Nicholson and Jessica Lange in 1981, the erotic effect of the 1946 version is much more powerful because the animal chemistry between John Garfield and Lana Turner is palpable even though they are fully clothed and nothing is visibly going on that the censor could possibly object to.

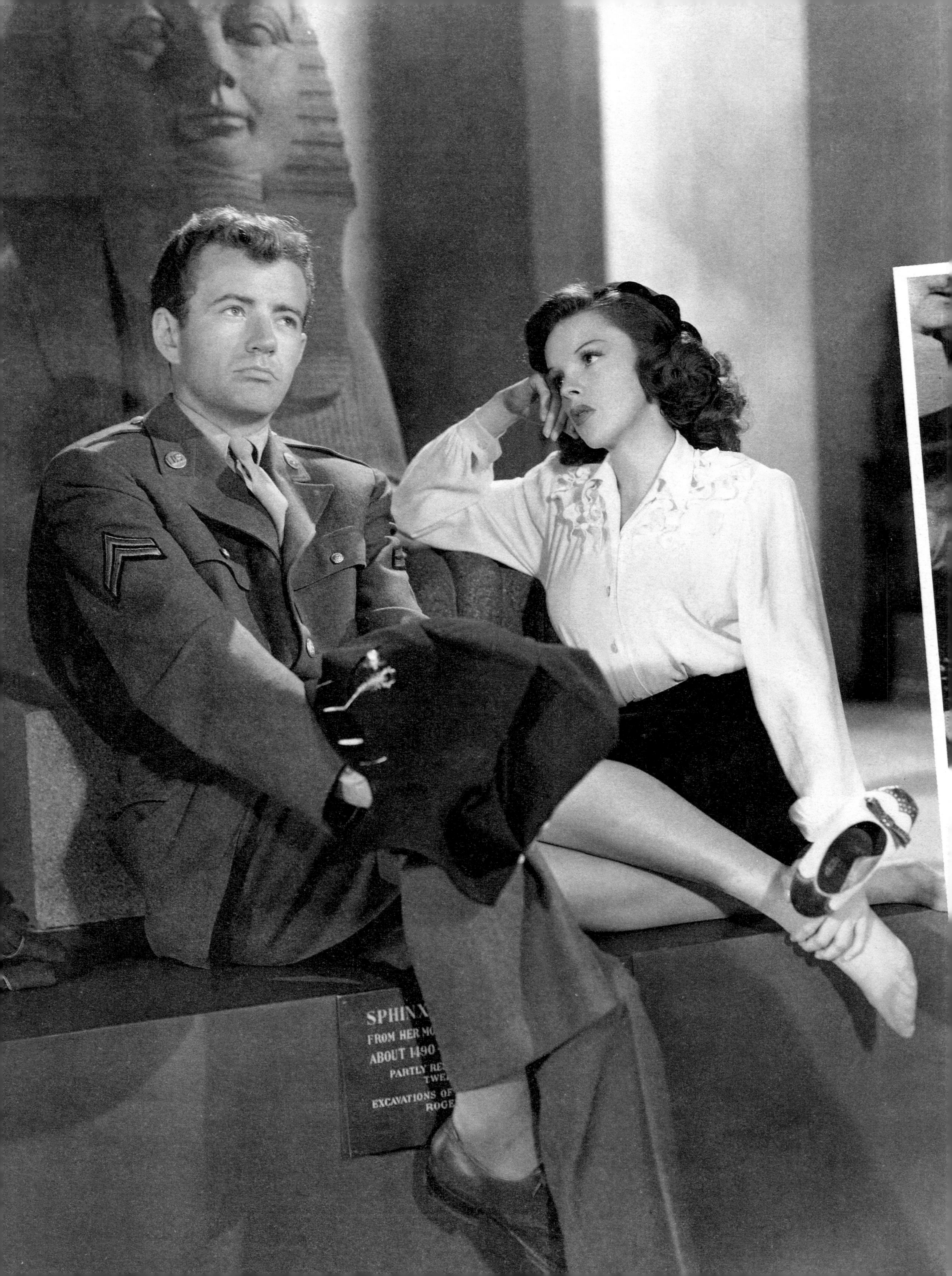
FROM HER
ABOUT 1490
PARTLY
EXCAVATIONS

Left: *Alice Maybery (Judy Garland), a New York girl, accidentally encounters Corporal Joe Allen (Robert Walker), an out-of-town soldier on 48 hours' leave, at Pennsylvania Station. She shows him the sights of the city, they part but miraculously meet again and impulsively decide to get married.* **The Clock** *(1945) was entirely a Hollywood studio movie, despite its New York atmosphere. Director Vincente Minnelli promptly married Judy Garland on its completion.*

Below: *Small-town boy Woodrow (Eddie Bracken), rejected by the army because of his non-stop sneezing, manages to return home to loud applause in* **Hail the Conquering Hero** *(1944), snappily directed by Preston Sturges, the decade's top comedy director.*

A lighter touch

Obviously not everything in the last two years of the war was entirely gloomy and negative – not even everything related to the war. There were still occasional comedies with some kind of war background, most notably Preston Sturges' **Hail the Conquering Hero** (1944), which uses the return to his home town of a totally undistinguished marine – invalided out of the service because he sneezes endlessly – as catalyst for a mordant picture of American small-town life. He is accepted as a hero, and the various reactions to his return and elevation to star status in the local community are sharply etched.

There was even room for a bittersweet romantic comedy like Vincente Minnelli's **The Clock** (1945), with Judy Garland and Robert Walker as war-crossed lovers who meet, marry, separate and eventually reunite in New York while he is waiting to be shipped abroad. The other images of GIs on furlough or invalided out were hardly more reassuring. In **I'll Be Seeing You** (1944) shell-shocked Joseph Cotten is encouraged to believe in himself again by the confidence of Ginger Rogers, only to be shattered when he finds that she is actually a jailbird let out briefly for good conduct. In **The Enchanted Cottage** (1945) a badly scarred veteran marries a very plain girl who has loved him all along, and to one another they become beautiful, though they learn the hard way that the miracle is for their eyes only. Both stories end happily, of course: the hero of **I'll Be Seeing You** manages finally to accept the heroine's plight and wait for her; the couple in **The Enchanted Cottage** manage to be content with their own view of life, without expecting insensitive outsiders to share it. This was fine in the movies, but suggested a widespread unwillingness on Hollywood's part to deal with the uncomfortable realities of war and its aftermath.

Road to laughter?

Indeed, escapism was in general the watchword, and not necessarily always the perverse escapism of *film noir* either: it might be into the cheery fantasy of the "Road" films, or the innocuous world of the MGM musical, or the nostalgia craze that had many studios rummaging through their old properties and creating new ones to take audiences back to the happy days before the Depression or even World War I.

It was never a classic period for comedy. Even the generally expert Frank Capra succumbed to the general frenzy in his version of the famous comedy of murders, **Arsenic and Old Lace** (made in 1942 but not released till 1944), directing even such an old and sure hand as Cary Grant to mug up a storm. However, the "Road" films, with the

Below and right: *Frank Capra's excellent **Arsenic and Old Lace** (1944) is a comedy of the unexpected. The murderesses are two dear, sweet old ladies who delight in inviting lonely men back to tea where they poison them with elderberry wine laced with arsenic. Their brother, who is so crazy that he thinks he is still fighting the Spanish-American war in Cuba, buries the bodies in the cellar. All goes well until their nephew (Cary Grant, below left) turns up with even more corpses. Priscilla Lane is a nervous witness to the goings-on, but Peter Lorre (far right) and Raymond Massey enjoy the mayhem with subterranean relish.*

The movie was an uncharacteristic work for the sentimentally populist Capra. Cary Grant reckons this is his favorite among all the films in which he has appeared.

inevitable threesome of Bob Hope, Bing Crosby and Dorothy Lamour, were a shining exception, being built up loosely but reliably on the interplay of the known screen personalities of the stars, with, of course, Hope and Crosby always fighting over the favors of the unimpressed Lamour and a long string of often faintly surrealist gags. The series, which had begun in 1940 with **Road to Singapore**, reached its apogee in 1945 with the fourth, **Road to Utopia**, though it staggered on through three more, the last and least of which was **Road to Hong Kong** (1962).

Most of the nostalgia-escapist films were musicals or semi-musicals, and many of the musicals were to some extent escapes into other periods. In **Cover Girl** (1944), for instance, a flashback allowed Rita Hayworth to play her own grandmother, a musical star of an earlier era, while modern times were reflected in a number of lively routines choreographed by co-star Gene Kelly and a song for Phil Silvers – "Who's Complaining?" – which referred humorously to wartime rationing.

Above: *"Like Webster's Dictionary we're Morocco bound", crooned Bob Hope (left) and Bing Crosby in **Road to Morocco** (1942). Crosby then sells Hope into slavery and woos Princess Shalmar (Dorothy Lamour) with the Johnny Burke/Jimmy Van Heusen number, "Moonlight Becomes You". Frank Butler and Don Hartman's witty script won an Academy Award nomination, and David Butler directed. This was the third in the very popular Paramount series of exotic excursions following trips to Singapore and Zanzibar. Next on the list is Yukon in the **Road to Utopia** (1945).*

Right: *Rita Hayworth poses for **Cover Girl** (1944), showing off her highly prized dancing legs. She started off as brunette Margarita Carmen Cansino, daughter of a Spanish dancer, switching to her mother's maiden name in 1937. Her husbands included Orson Welles and Aly Khan.*

Music hath charms

Musical biographies of George Gershwin (**Rhapsody in Blue**, 1945), of Texas Guinan, queen of twenties nightclubs (**Incendiary Blonde**, 1945) and of **The Dolly Sisters** (1945) often did not take the re-creation of their period backgrounds very seriously, but at least looked backwards lovingly. And then there was a whole group of affectionate pieces of period Americana, set off seemingly by the enormous success of Vincente Minnelli's exquisitely stylish **Meet Me in St Louis** (1944), which had Judy Garland growing up amid the preparations for the great St Louis Exposition of 1904.

Among the films that immediately followed it were **State Fair** (1945), a remake with a new score by Rodgers and Hammerstein; **Centennial Summer** (1946), with a new score by Jerome Kern; and **Margie** (1946), in which Jeanne Crain suffered the pains and pleasures of a twenties adolescence, with enough music to remove the film from harsh reality, if not quite enough to transform it into a proper musical.

Meet Me in St Louis (1944) was based on a nostalgic serial in the New Yorker by Sally Benson, recalling the 1904 World Exposition in St Louis. It follows the life of the Smith family through four seasons, from summer 1903 to spring 1904, finding romance and fighting off a proposed move to New York. The lead part of Esther is played by Judy Garland **left** whose closest confidante is her elder sister Rose (Lucille Bremer, **above**). Her little sister Tootie (Margaret O'Brien, **right**) performs "The Cakewalk" with her at their brother's birthday party.

Top right: The film nears its climax on Christmas Eve when Esther gets a longed-for proposal of marriage from the boy next door.

Above and right: *On the Town* (1949) originated early in 1944 with a ballet, Fancy Free, by composer Leonard Bernstein and choreographer Jerome Robbins, later to be associated with **West Side Story** (1961). This tale of three sailors on 24 hours' shoreleave in New York was expanded into a Broadway show by writers Betty Comden and Adolph Green, and became a big hit. MGM owned the film rights but was in no hurry to use them. Finally innovative producer Arthur Freed permitted Gene Kelly and his co-choreographer Stanley Donen to direct it as their first entire film together. There were compromises, however. Most of the ballet sequences were dropped; so was much of Bernstein's music, replaced by Roger Edens' simpler, more commercial tunes. These — and the urban setting — made a superb base for MGM artifice and streetwise wit.

The cast could not have been bettered: the three sailors, Chip (Frank Sinatra), Ozzie (Jules Munshin) and Gabey (Gene Kelly); their girls, man-eating cabbie Brunhilde Esterhazy (Betty Garrett), sexy anthropologist Claire Huddesen (Ann Miller) and demure "Miss Turnstiles" Ivy Smith (Vera-Ellen); not to mention Florence Bates as a hard-drinking dance teacher and Alice Pearce as a comic-pathetic wallflower.

The contemporary scene was not entirely neglected, even in "proper" musicals. There were still sterling, if geographically vague, attempts to cement pan-American relations, and even vaguer nods to the war effort. Carmen Miranda was let loose on **Greenwich Village** (1944), and sent out to cheer the troops in **Four Jills in a Jeep** (1944), along with Alice Faye, Betty Grable and the "four Jills" themselves, played by Kay Francis, Carole Landis, Martha Raye and Mitzi Mayfair. **Bathing Beauty** (1944), the vehicle that launched Esther Williams, the new aquatic sensation, also featured the frantic comedy of Red Skelton and Xavier Cugat and a slew of explosive Latins such as the "famous Columbian baritone" Carlos Ramirez.

Even the film most indicative of the shape of musicals to come, **Anchors Aweigh** (1945), though primarily about a couple of sailors on leave in Hollywood, also could not resist getting Gene Kelly mixed up choreographically with some cutely ethnic Mexican children. This was sidestepping the film's prophetic quality, however, which lay in the happy combination of Kelly and Frank Sinatra, with Kelly's inventive dance direction, which beckoned towards **Take Me Out to the Ball Game** (1948) and the most influential musical of the decade, **On the Town** (1949).

Back to Reality 1946-7

Chapter 4

Naturally, before movie-making was sufficiently organized and industrialized to have spawned the studio system, movies were made largely in real places, or at least in stage-like settings built in natural light. But the cinema of the twenties and thirties thrived on illusion: the studios were the dream factories, and it was very rarely thought necessary to take film units away from Los Angeles on expensive and hazardous location adventures. A few semi-documentary exceptions were well publicized, but in the main the attitude to locations was that of the veteran producer who said: "A rock is a rock and a tree is a tree: shoot it in Griffith Park." (Griffith Park being a large, open, hilly area in the center of Los Angeles.) Immediately after the end of the war in 1945 ideas really began to change.

Street life

It is not easy to pin down the origins of the move towards realism in Hollywood movies after 1945. The bandwagon got rolling with a film that came out late in 1945, **The House on 92nd Street**, a tough thriller about spies in New York. A few film-makers in Hollywood had previously insisted on using real locations to give an extra realistic dimension to their films, notably the great French director Jean Renoir on his first American film, **Swamp Water** (1941), shot largely in the South, and on **The Southerner** (1945), shot in California but well away from Hollywood.

The producer of **The House on 92nd Street**, Louis de Rochemont, was the first to bring public attention to urban location shooting. His background had been in **The March of Time**, a famous series of topical documentaries in the thirties, and in factual films made for the American government and the various armed services during the war. He therefore had principles about eliminating the falsity he sensed in most Hollywood films, which would happily re-create New York, London or Paris on the studio backlot, and have stars react to hazy back-projections shot by a second unit in places they had never been. Though **The House on 92nd Street** was shot by an accomplished studio director, Henry Hathaway, and was probably not much closer to reality than dozens of other spy films of that era, it did gain in vividness by the "authentication" of real places in the background, and, most important, was a box-office success.

Right: *Exiled French director Jean Renoir's most ''American'' film was* **The Southerner** *(1945), in which he tried to catch the essence of rural Texas by showing a year in the life of a family of tenant farmers. This shot shows the children, Jot (Jay Gilpin) and Daisy (Jean Vanderbilt), Grandma (Beulah Bondi), Nona (Betty Field) and Sam Tucker (Zachary Scott). Despite the cruel weather and a mean-minded neighbor, they manage to survive, just.*

Inventing the truth

This, of course, was what principally encouraged the others. "Shot on the streets where it really happened" became an easy publicity tag, applied rapidly to all sorts of things that probably never came near to happening anywhere. Mark Hellinger, another producer with a background in journalism, was quick to see the advantages, and after producing such defiantly unrealistic works as **Thank Your Lucky Stars** (1943), one of the all-star revues to entertain the forces, and **The Horn Blows at Midnight** (1945), another comedy about celestial interference in the affairs of mankind, he suddenly made a gritty, realistic thriller, extensively shot on location, out of Ernest Hemingway's short story **The Killers**. The 1946 film uses Hemingway's story in the opening sequence, and then goes on to invent its own explanations, loosely tied to the theme of restlessness among demobilized veterans and the problems of fitting into civilian life again. (The difficulties of the returning soldier often provided a jumping-off point for thriller plots at this time – usually when he found his wife had been unfaithful or his non-combatant partner had taken over his business in his absence.) **The Killers** was directed by Robert Siodmak and is an interesting fusion of *film noir* with location-shooting technique; so were several of his later films, such as **Cry of the City** (1948) and **Criss-Cross** (1949).

Top: *Betty Field and Zachary Scott in* **The Southerner** *(1945).*

Above: **The Killers** *(1946), which derived from a 1927 short story by Ernest Hemingway. Swede Lunn (Burt Lancaster) waits resignedly for the hitmen to kill him while gazing into the eyes of the attractive and ambiguous Kitty Collins (Ava Gardner).*

Right: *Kitty is sane, bad and dangerous to know – the classic* femme fatale *of the film noir. She plays the girlfriend of a gang-leader, persuading Swede to join the gang and double-cross them after a robbery. But then she double-crosses Swede, returning to her lover with the money so destroying Swede's will to live. The film was remade in 1964 with Lee Marvin, Ronald Reagan, and Angie Dickinson.*

Below: *Henry Hathaway's* **Call Northside 777** *(1948) is the story of an investigation: a crime reporter, McNeal (James Stewart), discovers that a Polish woman, Tillie Wiecek (Kasia Orzaewski), has scrubbed floors for 11 years to get enough money to prove her imprisoned son Frank not guilty of murder. Impressed by her faith, McNeal takes up the task and a newspaper photograph wins the day.*

In the next couple of years both Louis de Rochemont and Mark Hellinger continued to develop the same kind of film and make capital out of location vividness: de Rochemont produced **13 Rue Madeleine** (1946) and **Boomerang** (1947), and Hellinger produced **Brute Force** (1947) and **The Naked City** (1948) before his premature death in 1947. By this time, too, influence had begun to come from another source: Italian neo-realism. This movement had originated in economic necessity. Towards the end of the war the Italian film industry virtually closed down as the major studios were marooned in fighting zones and physical resources for film-making were reduced to an absolute minimum. The only way of making films at all was by improvising on real locations. The first film made this way, Roberto Rossellini's **Rome, Open City** (1945), immediately won international acclaim, as did his **Paisan** and Vittorio De Sica's **Shoeshine** (both 1946) and **Bicycle Thieves** (1948) and the work of many of their contemporaries.

Though many Hollywood stalwarts would claim to be indifferent to highbrow critical enthusiasm, provided their films were successful at the box office, the younger generation of directors emerging in the late forties hankered more after critical laurels as well as commercial credibility, and accordingly the lesson of Italian neo-realism, reinforcing the ideas of de Rochemont and Hellinger, was not lost on them.

The documentary touch

There followed in Hollywood a spate of allegedly semi-documentary dramas, sometimes made by old dogs like Hathaway who had learnt new tricks (**Kiss of Death,** 1947; **Call Northside 777,** 1948) or William Keighley (**The Street With No Name**, 1948), but more often by newcomers. De Rochemont and Hellinger's own productions helped the careers of such new directors as Elia Kazan (**Boomerang**) and Jules Dassin (**Brute Force, The Naked City**), shortly to be

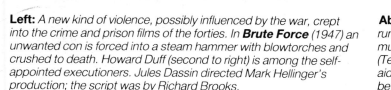

Left: *A new kind of violence, possibly influenced by the war, crept into the crime and prison films of the forties. In **Brute Force** (1947) an unwanted con is forced into a steam hammer with blowtorches and crushed to death. Howard Duff (second to right) is among the self-appointed executioners. Jules Dassin directed Mark Hellinger's production; the script was by Richard Brooks.*

Above and top: *The Naked City (1948), which spawned a long-running television series. A detective (Don Taylor), investigating the murder of a blonde, finds himself at the mercy of a fitness-freak killer (Ted de Corsia) and ends up by chasing the villain over a bridge, aided by the fast firing cops. This film was another collaboration between Hellinger and Dassin.*

Below: *In **Boomerang** (1947) John Waldron (Arthur Kennedy) comes under suspicion for the murder of a priest in a Connecticut town (the film was shot on location in Stamford). Here he is given the third degree by Lieutenant White (Karl Malden, center) and Sergeant Dugan (Darry Kelley) but claims he was at the movies when the killing occurred. "Which one?", snaps White. The alibi falls down but the case still remains unsolved – like the real-life one on which it was based. The director Elia Kazan, who lived not far away, was able to give a grim reality to this story of civic corruption. Soon afterwards, he helped found the famous Actors Studio.*

followed into the big time by Nicholas Ray (**They Drive By Night**, 1948), Fred Zinnemann (**The Search**, 1948) and Joseph Losey (**The Boy With Green Hair**, 1948), all inspired at that time by a realist approach. In the long run, location-shooting became the norm in Hollywood, whether or not the subject was realistic or had any sort of social comment to make.

In the two years after the war, though, location shooting was still new and exciting, and was certainly promoted as such. In some respects it appeared diametrically opposed to the reigning genre, *film noir*, with its carefully controlled visual world of neo-Expressionistic studio-sets and lighting. But in other ways the distinction was not so clear as it seemed. The general tone of most of the location-shot films was tough and gloomy: exposing social injustice in such films as **Boomerang**, a grim, downbeat version of a real-life investigation into the New England murder of an Episcopalian minister, and Edward Dmytryk's **Crossfire** and Kazan's **Gentlemen's Agreement**, which probed the anti-Semitism latent beneath the cool, liberal exterior of American life. But **Crossfire** is particularly difficult to categorize: most of the key scenes take place at night, and the atmosphere of obsessional corruption that surrounds the character soon revealed as the Jew-killer is very typically *film noir*, while a number of the lesser characters are played by actors like Gloria Grahame and Paul Kelly, whose usual stamping-ground was the *film noir* proper. Nor is

Crossfire, like 1947's **Gentlemen's Agreement** (in which Gregory Peck masquerades as a Jew for a series of articles he is writing and finds out about anti-Semitism the hard way), overtly didactic: it makes its social point through atmosphere and psychology of the kinds that crop up throughout *film noir*.

Black satin

That movement, of course, continued on its unmerry way through 1946 and 1947. Some of the best examples, indeed, come from this time. Hitchcock's finest contribution to the genre, **Notorious** (1946) is a dark love story – in which the heroine (Ingrid Bergman) has to go to the edge of death itself in order to convince the hero (Cary Grant) that she loves him and is worthy of his love – disguised as a Rio-based espionage story about refugee Nazis. Rita Hayworth was incarnated as an especially bewitching *femme fatale* in Charles Vidor's **Gilda** (1946), another Latin American excursion in which she breaks up the attachment between her ex-lover Glenn Ford and her picturesquely sadistic present husband George Macready, as well as performing the extraordinary glove-striptease as she sings "Put the Blame on Mame" while clad in sheer black satin. A bit later, in 1948, her husband Orson Welles cut off her red locks and cast her as a blond and reptilian temptress, opposite himself, in his darkly haunting **The Lady from Shanghai**.

Left and below: *"There never was another woman like* **Gilda**" *(1946). Nor like red-headed Rita Hayworth. She sang "Put the Blame on Mame, Boys" while stripping only her gloves – a performance she parodied in* **Pal Joey** *(1957) with "Zip".*

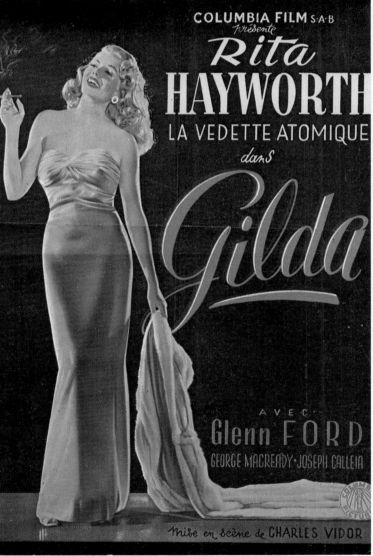

COLUMBIA FILM S·A·B
présente
RITA HAYWORTH
LA VEDETTE ATOMIQUE
dans
Gilda

AVEC
Glenn FORD
GEORGE MACREADY · JOSEPH CALLEIA

Mise en scène de CHARLES VIDOR

These films were made by dabblers in the form. Regular experts continued to work in their established fashion, too. Robert Siodmak made **The Dark Mirror** (1946), which featured a psychiatrist hero and twins (both Olivia de Havilland), one good, one bad – ah, but which is which? John Brahm went on from **Hangover Square** to **The Locket** (1946), an even more overwrought psychological drama about a beautiful bride (Laraine Day) who is an amnesiac and possibly a murderess. Fritz Lang continued his collaboration with Joan Bennett in **The Secret Beyond the Door** (1948), creating yet more dark dreams and forgotten mysteries. And *films noirs* as accomplished as **The Strange Love of Martha Ivers** (1946), **Dark Passage, The Unsuspected** and **Nightmare Alley** (all 1947), were produced on cue by solid craftsmen as various and versatile as, respectively, Delmer Daves, Michael Curtiz, Lewis Milestone and Edmund Goulding, all willingly and very capably falling in with the mood of the moment. Charles Chaplin meanwhile made the very, very black comedy **Monsieur Verdoux** (1947), in which his dapper wife-murderer replaced forever the little tramp.

Below: *Twin sisters, good and evil (ego and id?), became a popular symbol of psychological or moral ambiguity in the Freud-conscious forties. Director Robert Siodmak, having tried it out with Maria Montez in* **Cobra Woman** *(1944), gave it another whirl with Olivia de Havilland in* **The Dark Mirror** *(1946). Here is both of her. Which is guilty?*

Right: *The police lieutenant tries to find out by sifting through the evidence. In this case the paranoid Terry (Olivia de Havilland) can be trapped only by psychological testing according to the principles established by psychiatrist Lew Ayres.*

GI Joe comes home

Life, on the outside, continued as real and earnest as ever. By now the men who had served overseas were back in civilian life and having problems, as Hollywood reflected. In **Cornered** (1945), **The Blue Dahlia** (1946) and **Ride the Pink Horse** (1947), for instance, the hero is a returning GI who finds that back home there is something to sort out and someone to avenge – in the first two his wife has been murdered, in the third his best friend – and sets off through the night-world of *film noir* to do what he has to do. The fact that he is a GI back from war was irrelevant, however, and very few films faced up to the real questions of readjustment to civilian life. Those that did were frequently accused of returning culpably soft answers. The most famous, and most argued-over instance, was **The Best Years of Our Lives** (1946), produced by Samuel Goldwyn, directed by William Wyler, scripted by Robert Sherwood (from a verse novel, oddly enough), photographed by Gregg Toland (most famous for **Citizen Kane**) and starring a range of old and new stars. The film was immensely successful with critics and at the

box-office, cut a swathe through the year's Oscars, and was apparently loved by all. Then the reaction set in: it was accused of sweetening and sentimentalizing the book, of being hollow and pretentious, academic, unrealistic and out of touch with the present.

There is, undeniably, some truth in all of these strictures, but there was something new and unexpected about the film. Though the principal married couple is embodied by big established stars, Fredric March and Myrna Loy, and a newer arrival Dana Andrews, who plays the least satisfied war veteran (less even, curiously, than the genuinely handless Harold Russell), they do not, as stars, carry the film: they are used primarily as actors who are more or less at home in their roles. It was the beginning of the transition to the new kind of star who came in with the fifties – the kind who was too late to be systematically built up by a studio and have his or her own unquestioning following. The new breed of star had to make it performance by performance, one by one.

Although the star system was changing, for the moment you would not notice any change. Clark Gable was back, along with James Stewart, Robert Taylor and Henry Fonda, and none of them seemed to have too much trouble slipping again into their appointed places in the Hollywood hierarchy. There may have been some momentary uncertainty, perhaps, but major box-office success, as when James Stewart teamed up with Hitchcock for **Rope** (1948), and Robert Taylor got into fancy dress for **Quo Vadis** (1951), indicated that such stars were still as popular as ever. Others, however, were on their way out. Greer Garson proved more vulnerable than her beau, Gable, in **Adventure** (1945); Alice Faye was a falling star at Fox and her replacement, Betty Grable, was also a threat. And if Joan Crawford was riding high in her new career away from MGM at Warners following **Mildred Pierce**, Bette Davis was nearing the end of her fabulous first career at the same studio and being pushed into more and more unsuitable vehicles – before she bounced back in **All About Eve** (1950). Contracts were up, and stars like Veronica Lake and Ann Sheridan (the "oomph girl") were cast adrift far more disastrously than Bette Davis. Among the men who had not gone to war the longest established stars seemed the most secure: no one was really challenging the position of such pre-war favorites as Gary Cooper, Cary Grant, Spencer Tracy, James Cagney or Humphrey Bogart, and when the crop of new stars like Richard Widmark, Burt Lancaster, Kirk Douglas, Montgomery Clift and Robert Mitchum came up after the war, they were of a different enough generation not to provide direct competition.

Left: *Chaplin's **Monsieur Verdoux** (1947), the story of a ladykiller, was based on an idea by Orson Welles and on the infamous Landru case.*

Right: *A production shot of Lewis Milestone (leaning on camera) directing Lizabeth Scott in **The Strange Love of Martha Ivers** (1946) for Paramount.*

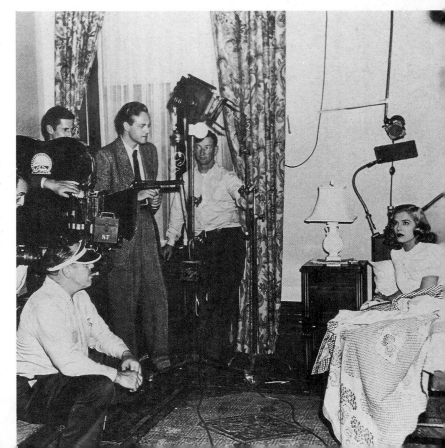

Creative lull?

What is notable in the immediately post-war years is a certain slackening of creative energy in Hollywood. Perhaps Hollywood had been having it too easy in the war years: after the nasty economic shocks caused by the advent of war in Europe, attendances for the movies had been soaring, and 1946 was indeed the most profitable year in the history of the American film industry. Television was yet a minor domestic toy, which could never rival the wonders of the big screen in the movie palace, while moves to break up the industry's production/distribution/exhibition monopoly via anti-trust laws were still to become a reality.

But if this was paradise, it turned out to be a fool's paradise. There were indications of disturbance already: industrial unrest in the studio unions in 1945 (with an eight-month closure in some cases), and in the laboratories in 1946, meant increasing costs and greater uncertainty. But Hollywood's real problems began with the imposition of a 75 per cent tax on foreign films by the British government in 1947. Britain was still the biggest single foreign market, so this cut foreign profits by nearly three-quarters, and the counter-move to boycott British markets altogether was only self-defeating. A sudden slump meant the elimination of many of the luxury trimmings that had always characterized Hollywood movies: a reduction of studio staff, a general tightening of belts and a new emphasis on efficiency in production. This mood also helped to reorientate Hollywood in the direction of location realism, small-scale production, and the encouragement of newer and less expensive talent. Films were in general less glossy, less inclined to conspicuous consumption, and more likely (by a somewhat obscure connexion of ideas) to have social content of some kind.

Red scare

To add to Hollywood's difficulties at this time, the House UnAmerican Activities Committee (HUAC) which, representing interests lying dormant since the preservation of neutrality had ceased to be an issue in 1941, sprang into life again in 1947 with new vigor, this time pursuing evidence of Communist infiltration into Hollywood. Since many people in the industry had flirted with left-wing politics in their youth, or belonged to Russian war-aid committees and even made pro-Russian films like **North Star** and **Mission to Moscow** (both 1943) when the Soviets were America's allies, this was often difficult to disprove. The general assumption of the committee was that you were guilty until you proved yourself innocent by suitable self-abasement and the naming of names.

The immediate result was, to put it mildly, a very nervous time in Hollywood, and the almost instant production of a group of vociferously anti-Communist films. Blacklists burgeoned, and lots of old personal scores were settled behind the scenes with secret denunciations. There was also, inevitably, the beginning of a significant brain-drain from Hollywood, as many who feared being witch-hunted left for Europe. In 1947 this was merely a trickle; by

Below: *The notorious communistic sympathies of studio bosses Jack L. Warner and his brothers emerged all too clearly in* **Mission to Moscow** *(1943), based on the memoirs of former ambassador Joseph E. Davies. Here Davies (Walter Huston) listens intently to the views of Comrade Stalin (Mannart Kippen) while the Soviet president (Vladimir Sokoloff) looks on benignly. The House UnAmerican Activities Committee did not like it at all.*

Above: *The Outlaw* was completed in 1941, briefly shown in 1943, given a limited release in 1946 (GB, 1947) but was not generally available until 1950. Jane Russell, seen here with Jack Buetel as Billy the Kid, fared the best, emerging from the film as a star.

Right: The classic RKO poster marking the film's general release. Jane Russell, as the bosomy Rio, actually figured rather little in the plot, which mostly revolved around a protracted contest for a stolen horse between Billy the Kid and Doc Holliday (Walter Huston), egged on by Pat Garrett (Thomas Mitchell). Howard Hughes directed after firing Hawks.

1949 it had become a flood – and worse was to come in the fifties with the arrival on the scene of Senator Joseph McCarthy.

All these disparate factors contributed to the instability of the studios themselves, which had for some years seemed a fixed and unchangeable quantity in Hollywood and American film-making. In 1946 the long-established Universal threw in its lot with the newer International Pictures to become Universal-International. David O. Selznick was making fewer and fewer films of his own, and finding the distribution company he had set up cumbersome and with little product to sell.

Howard Hughes had taken a fancy, during the making and remaking of **The Outlaw** (1941-50), which launched his new discovery Jane Russell, to control the whole film-making and marketing process, and had begun negotiating to buy RKO outright, a deal finally concluded in 1948. And other studios were in the throes of change, even the sacrosanct MGM, where Louis B. Mayer was gradually having to countenance the production of films that clashed with his own preference for sanitized, apple pie family entertainment. When the liberal Dore Schary was brought in as production head, with all the progressive ideas he had been trying to develop in pre-Hughes RKO, the old MGM image was changed forever. It had not yet lost quite all of its "more stars than there are in heaven", but most of them were fading fast. And if even MGM was changing, what was then left in Hollywood to rely on?

Brave New World 1948-9

Chapter 5

A practical belief has always been built into the Hollywood way of life – everyone knows that what goes up must come down, nothing lasts forever. This kind of pattern was expected in the career of the individual star, director or writer; in particular cycles of film types and subjects; even, perhaps in the history of major studios and production companies. And in the forties it happened to the industry as a whole. The decade started with an alarming slump due to the loss of European markets at the outbreak of World War II, although Hollywood managed to climb out of it partly because the entry of America into the war boosted the home market. There were war workers needing to be taken out of themselves and women and children feeling the absence of boyfriends, husbands and fathers.

Then in 1947 the roof fell in. Though something akin to panic had hit Hollywood, it was not necessarily apparent to the outside world: pictures, the publicity kept trumpeting, were bigger and better than ever, and more intelligent. Economic necessity pointed the way towards smaller films; depending on strong ideas rather than high production values, and so provided an opening for younger directors and writers with things to say. Accordingly new producers addressed themselves to social problems rather than, like Val Lewton in the war years, questions of style. Dore Schary at RKO, and from 1948 at MGM, specialized in small-budget and then progressively more expensive films with some kind of crusading point to be made. In 1948 an ex-writer and film editor called Stanley Kramer made a modest period piece, **So This Is New York**, as his first independent production, then went on immediately to make **Champion**, about corruption in boxing; **House of the Brave**, concerning the breakdown of a black soldier through fear and anger over race prejudice back home; and **The Men**, about paraplegic veterans – a film that gave Marlon Brando his first leading film role. All of these films were solemn, literary and rather stodgy, but forced critics and at least a segment of the public to approve of them for their good intentions, and all of them went to swell the numbers of films in the currently fashionable social-problem cycle.

It was fortunate that some more experienced producers, like Darryl F. Zanuck, back from the war and in charge of 20th Century-Fox, should also be attracted to the idea of films that made some serious comment on social questions of current interest, and that some really talented directors like Elia Kazan and Fred Zinnemann should also be that way inclined, since no cycle could live by good intentions alone.

Right: *Future megastar Marlon Brando seen here as a wheelchair-bound ex-soldier in* **The Men** *(1950) with Teresa Wright as his girlfriend.*

Far right: *Pinky Johnson (Jeanne Crain) in* **Pinky** *(1949) with Granny Dicey Johnson (Ethel Waters) looking heavenward for help.*

Right: *Jean Simmons, an established star in Britain, made her first big impact on Hollywood in Otto Preminger's* **Angel Face** *(1952), strong in emotion and plot. Simmons plays Diane, who adores her father (Herbert Marshall) but detests her stepmother, whom she tries to kill — and eventually succeeds, but at the same time accidentally killing her father. Tried for murder with her accomplice Frank, she marries him, and gets off, but the plan backfires when he rejects her. In revenge she kills both Frank and herself in another crash. A fifties film with a forties flavor.*

It took a MAN to handle
Her Kind of Love...

JEAN SIMMONS
First Film
from Hollywood

...But
no one
could handle
her kind of
MURDER!

HOWARD HUGHES
presents
ROBERT
MITCHUM
JEAN
SIMMONS
ANGEL FACE
co-starring MONA FREEMAN HERBERT MARSHALL with LEON AMES BARBARA O'NEIL
Produced and Directed by OTTO PREMINGER. Screenplay by: FRANK NUGENT and OSCAR MILLARD.
From The Showmanship Company
RKO RADIO PICTURES

Left: *Claude Jarman Jr makes friends with a fawn in* **The Yearling** *(1946), adapted from Marjorie Kinnan Rawlings' novel by Greta Garbo's favorite director, Clarence Brown. The boy won a special "child actor" Oscar.*

Ultimately, this type of film, so commonly seen from 1947 to 1950, depended not on the seriousness of their message but on their qualities as movie entertainment. But there was a disconcerting tendency on Hollywood's part to see all problems as interchangeable: the homosexual in the novel on which **Crossfire** was based could be changed into a Jew because that made the issue more acceptable in 1947, just as readily as the Jew in the original play **House of the Brave** could be changed into a black because in 1949 the Jewish problem was less newsworthy than the "black" problem.

A question of color

Racial problems were a burning issue in films in 1949. De Rochemont's contribution to the cycle, **Lost Boundaries**, and Zanuck's **Pinky** (directed by Kazan after John Ford left the production) concerned blacks passing for white who came to face the necessity of being true to themselves and finding their proper place in society. The stars concerned – Mel Ferrer in **Lost Boundaries**, Jeanne Crain in **Pinky** – could hardly look whiter if they tried, and while that is the essence of their characters' particular problem, it does also obscure the issue by making it almost entirely psychological. It also ensured that the racial subject matter did little for black actors. James Edwards in **House of the Brave** approximated closely to white standards of handsomeness, and so did the long-established Lena Horne and the next black stars to make it big, Harry Belafonte and Dorothy Dandridge in 1954's **Carmen Jones**.

But at least one very dynamic and quite obviously black actor was emerging: Sidney Poitier played his first major film role in the most uncompromising and intelligent of the first black cycle, Joseph L. Mankiewicz's **No Way Out**, an unsparing picture of reasoning racial bigotry that brought up the tail end of the series in 1950.

The best film of the group seemed to be there almost by accident. No doubt **Intruder in the Dust** was made at MGM largely because of Dore Schary's liberalizing presence, but in most respects it belonged to a long line of well-upholstered MGM adaptations of best-sellers and modern classics, rather self-consciously sold as such. "Class" was written all over this version of William Faulkner's novel, directed by Clarence Brown. It concerned a proud and intransigent old black farmer (Juano Hernandez) who refuses to "act black" when accused of murdering a white man, and creates more resentment by not bowing to the white bigots than by the crime of which he is unjustly accused. The main emphasis of the film is on the white boy who is one of the few to befriend and defend him, and probably the principal motive for making the film was to provide a suitable vehicle for MGM's most important juvenile star of the time, Claude Jarman Jr, who had won a special Academy Award for **The Yearling** in 1946.

Right: *Sorry Wrong Number* (1948) became the vehicle for a bravura performance by Barbara Stanwyck as a wealthy Sutton Place invalid, confined to bed with only the telephone as her outside contact. She becomes aware that she is the intended victim of a murder plot and desperately tries to summon help, at first not knowing who is behind the contract. But her struggles inexorably end in failure – flimsy expensive lace cannot protect her from the merciless leather glove of the assassin.

Husband Burt Lancaster, who was behind it all, at the last minute regrets his murderous plan as the police close in **below**. The old Hollywood system rarely allowed the murderer to succeed.

Above: *Celeste Holm (left) and Olivia de Havilland (second from right) as inmates of a hellish lunatic asylum in* **The Snake Pit** *(1949). Strong stuff in its day, it was said to have affected attitudes to mental illness and its treatment. But compared with the later revelations of ex-film star Frances Farmer of conditions around the same time, it now seems relatively tame. However,* **Sorry Wrong Number** *and* **The Snake Pit** *did give an undeniable and welcome touch of class to the otherwise merely competent (on the whole) career of Russian-born Anatole Litvak. His two somewhat divergent gifts, for documentary and for working well with top actresses, came together very effectively at this point.*

The darkest hour...

By 1948 the *film noir* cycle was drawing to a close, though there were occasional stragglers like Preminger's **Angel Face** or **Vicky**, a remake of 1941's **I Wake Up Screaming** with a significant change of emphasis. Some of the best examples in the late forties came from emigré directors still working in Hollywood. Anatole Litvak made two of the blackest contributions, both featuring virtuoso female performances in the central role. Barbara Stanwyck was the rich, menaced invalid whose only contact with the outside world is by telephone in **Sorry Wrong Number** (1948); and Olivia de Havilland was the woman who goes through the nightmare of a lunatic asylum in **The Snake Pit** (1949). The Austrian Max Ophüls was in Hollywood for a long time before he got a chance to show what he could do with the moody and elegant Viennese period piece **Letter from an Unknown Woman** in 1948, and the two distinctly black films he made afterwards, **Caught** and **The Reckless Moment**, both of which, as the titles indicate, picture a deterministic world where a momentary error can trap one for life.

An unexpected recruit to the ranks of *film noir* directors was King Vidor, famed since the twenties as one of Hollywood's great humanists. Possibly working on Selznick's sadistic super-Western **Duel in the Sun** in 1947 helped to change his view of things, but in 1949 he came up with two astonishing works, **The Fountainhead**, based on Ayn Rand's novel, about a megalomaniac architect (Gary Cooper) who reserves the right to destroy his own buildings if they do not come up to his required standards, and **Beyond the Forest**, Bette Davis' last film on her Warners contract. This had her wearing a Charles Addams fright-wig to portray a mid-western Emma Bovary who destroys everything about her to get on that train to Chicago but never quite succeeds. Meanwhile, less challenging was William Wyler's first film since **The Best Years of Our Lives**, a highly polished version of **The Heiress**, the matinee melodrama Ruth and Augustus Goetz had extracted from Henry James' richly ambiguous novel **Washington Square**.

Right and far right: *Beyond the Forest* (1949). Is Rosa Moline (Bette Davis) a mid-Western Emma Bovary or a burnt-out Warners star camping it up on her last assignment? Dr Lewis Moline (Joseph Cotten) puts up with it all, even when she practically falls under the outgoing Chicago train!

Below: *Duel in the Sun* (1947) with Jennifer Jones as the half-caste Pearl Chavez, who comes between two brothers, Lewt (Gregory Peck) and Jesse, played by hard-working Joseph Cotten (absent from this lobby card). Its violent climax led to its nickname, "Lust in the Dust".

This page: *Adam's Rib* *(1949) was the first and possibly the best of George Cukor's half-dozen comedy collaborations with the husband and wife team of writer-director Garson Kanin and writer-actress Ruth Gordon: perhaps this was because it was the only one to include Spencer Tracy and Katharine Hepburn and Judy Holliday instead of just one or at most two of them.*
The plot has a delightful range of comic possibilities with Adam Bonner (Tracy) as an assistant DA and his wife Amanda (Hepburn) as the defence lawyer in the case of a housewife so angered by seeing her husband with another woman that she takes a pot shot at him.

Left and below: *As the courtroom and domestic tensions increase in **Adam's Rib**; Amanda consoles herself in a mild flirtation with an old beau, Kip Lurie. Adam reacts violently, even though he has just been lambasting the defendant for behaving in the same jealous way. The movie delightfully explores sexist bias, even at one point dressing Doris as a man and her husband as a woman. Tom Ewell **below** on the carpet.*

Something old, something new

Other stalwarts were learning new tricks, or satisfactorily dusting off old forgotten ones. George Cukor, an accomplished director during MGM's heyday, suddenly showed a quite unsuspected flair for location shooting and the brisk, modern New York-based comedies written by Garson Kanin and Ruth Gordon. **Adam's Rib** (1949) was the first of a succession of hits starring Spencer Tracy and Katharine Hepburn or Judy Holliday or (in this case) both.

John Ford, whose version of the gunfight at the OK Corral myth, **My Darling Clementine** (1946), with Henry Fonda as Wyatt Earp and Victor Mature as Doc Holliday, was eccentric in its scope and star-power, fully revived the Western in the late forties with his "cavalry trilogy". **Fort Apache** (1948), **She Wore a Yellow Ribbon** (1949) and **Rio Grande** (1950) were films that poetically harnessed landscape – that of Ford's beloved Monument Valley – to storyline and also got the best from the director's stock company. They also consolidated John Wayne as a Western hero of noble stature – as did

Below and below right: *The battle of nature and culture is savagely taken up in* **My Darling Clementine** *(1946), whether on the battlefield of the OK Corral, the final showdown between the law-abiding Earps and the untamed Clantons or in the tonsorial parlor where Wyatt Earp (Henry Fonda) has his locks disciplined by the barber (Ben Hall). The good guys of Tombstone are: John Simpson (Russell Simpson), Doc Holliday (Victor Mature), Morgan Earp (Ward Bond), a decoy, and finally Wyatt himself. They will kill all but Old Man Clanton, played by Walter Brennan, who virtually commits suicide by drawing on Wyatt as he rides away. According to director John Ford, the real Wyatt Earp told him the whole story back in the early days, so it's practically a documentary!*

Howard Hawks' cattledrive epic **Red River** (1948), a masterpiece of storytelling. Ford's **The Wagonmaster** (1950), about a group of Mormon settlers heading West, was another excellent Western that helped usher the genre into its finest decade – although political overtones and psychological complexity would greatly alter its shape during the fifties.

Another great veteran who ended the decade by reverting to tried and trusted methods was Cecil B. DeMille. He had begun the forties with a spectacular "Western", **North West Mounted Police** (1940), starring Gary Cooper and Paulette Goddard, who also appeared together in the 1947 DeMille epic, **Unconquered**. He also made **Reap the Wild Wind** (1942), a Georgia-based seafaring drama with Goddard, Ray Milland, John Wayne and a giant squid, and his own flag-waving tribute to wartime American heroism, reliably personified by Cooper, in **The Story of Dr Wassell** (1944). But in 1949 DeMille fell back on the old formula of sex-and-sadism with a biblical excuse when he revamped an old thirties project as **Samson and Delilah**. If the idea of Hedy Lamarr and Victor Mature in the title roles filled the critics with unseemly mirth, the film at least reasserted DeMille's sure grasp of the taste of the public at large.

The last of Sturges

Comedies were, as usual, a staple of this period, though sadly the great comic discovery of the forties, writer/director Preston Sturges, was already burning himself out. His last satisfactory film was **Unfaithfully Yours** (1948), in which the conductor of an orchestra fantasizes various solutions to his current marital problems during a concert – and then tries confusedly to put all his ideas simultaneously into practice. Sturges' last Hollywood film, a Betty Grable vehicle called **The Beautiful Blonde From Bashful Bend** (1949), pleased no one. Frank Capra was nearing the end of his effective career. After a big success with his post-war comeback film, **It's a Wonderful Life** (1946), a Christmas fantasy in which a popular local hero (James Stewart) learns – with the help of an angel – how his little town would have suffered had he never lived, Capra changed his tone to something much tougher and more ruthless in **State of the Union** (1948), a political satire tailored to the requirements of the star team of Tracy and Hepburn.

Right: *Paulette Goddard was rather good at being delightfully no-good and Chaplin had encouraged her spirited New York-Jewish wit. Having missed out on the part of Scarlett O'Hara, she played a Georgian belle in C. B. DeMille's* **Reap the Wild Wind** *(1942), fought over by John Wayne and Ray Milland. However, she misses out on this poster, too, being supplanted by the saucy Susan Hayward.*

Below and far right: *Swiss-fathered Victor Mature and Viennese Hedy Lamarr make an odd yet appropriate couple as* **Samson and Delilah** *in DeMille's 1949 epic, which took a very respectable $11.5m in US rentals alone. Mature is big and hunky yet curiously soft and self-deprecating with an almost feminine streak. Lamarr is a hard little beauty, capable of cruelty. Ergo, perfect casting for a sado-masochistic biblical fantasy.*

104

Below: *Spencer Tracy and Katharine Hepburn made the fifth of their nine films together in 1948. Its punning title, **State of the Union**, suggests a conflation of domestic and political themes. An estranged wife (Hepburn) rejoins her businessman husband (Tracy) when he is persuaded to run for the Presidency by a rich, ruthless lady newspaper publisher.*

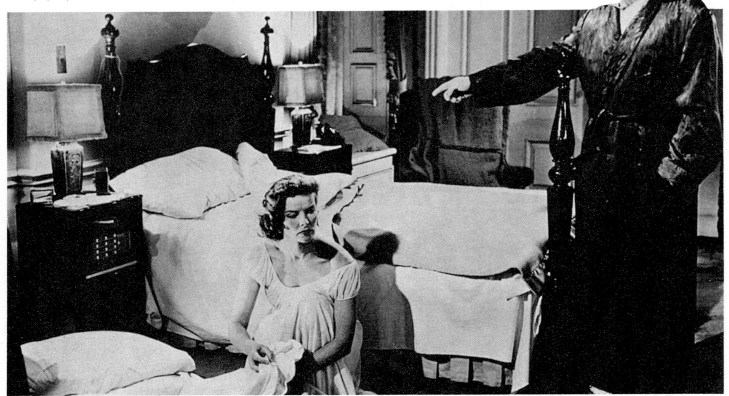

Right: *John Wayne and Oliver Hardy in* **The Fighting Kentuckian** *(1949). Wayne was still the main prop of Republic Pictures, producing this one too, and accepting the inevitable Czech ex-ice skater Vera Ralston (not shown) as his co-star.*
Ollie's screen partnership with Stan had virtually ended, and in effect both were finished after 1940. Ollie made his last Hollywood film in 1950; the duo made their last in 1951. Ollie died in 1957, Stan in 1965.

Above: *Marilyn Monroe's first major role was not at her "home" studio, 20th Century-Fox, where she started and ended her fifteen-year career, but at Columbia.* **Ladies of the Chorus** *(1948) was the only film she made there – it gave her (center right) a glamorous mother (Adele Jergens, center left) less than nine years her senior. Unnerved by this anomaly (her real-life mother was problem enough) she falters in her pursuit of a rich husband . . . but only briefly.*

Left: *The Beautiful Blonde from Bashful Bend (1949) was not one of Betty Grable's best films and still less one of Preston Sturges' best. He was more at home with the raucous Betty Hutton; and this was to be his last American film. Grable (pointing the finger at Cesar Romero) is a tough saloon dancer out West, too handy with a gun. When she accidentally shoots a sheriff, she finds it convenient to hide out for a while and allow herself to be mistaken for a schoolmistress.*

The shape of things to come

Other comic standbys were also vanishing from the scene. The **Bullfighters** (1945) was the last Hollywood film to star Laurel and Hardy together, though Hardy appeared with John Wayne in **The Fighting Kentuckian** in 1949 and made a final bow with Laurel in the French **Robinson Crusoeland** (1950). The last film in which Groucho, Chico and Harpo Marx appeared together was **Love Happy** (1950). This film showed off, in a short but spectacular bit part, a pretty young blonde – lusted after by Groucho – who in 1948 had played her first leading role in a small feature called **Ladies of the Chorus**. Her name was Marilyn Monroe, and very soon everyone in the world would have heard it. Already in 1950 she was being featured in major new films by the two most important directorial talents to confirm their Hollywood posititon in the late forties, John Huston and Joseph L. Mankiewicz.

Immediately before putting Monroe, as a gangster's moll, in the crime thriller **The Asphalt Jungle** (1950), Huston had made one of his best-respected misfires, **We Were Strangers** (1948), about a group of revolutionaries in Cuba, and one of his big successes, **The Treasure of the Sierra Madre** (1949), a harshly ironic prospecting adventure story starring Humphrey Bogart and Oscar-winning Walter Huston, the director's father. Mankiewicz, who gave Monroe a small part as the girl on George Sanders' arm in the classic bitchery of **All About Eve** (1950), had made a highly effective thriller/family drama, **House of Strangers** (1949); a contribution to the group of films concerned with racial prejudice, **No Way Out** (1950); and, most successfully of all, his brilliant episodic comedy drama **A Letter to Three Wives** (1949), in which he developed the elegant, witty "talk film" that was his speciality. Here three wives at a picnic receive a letter from an absentee fourth announcing she has run off with one of their husbands – but whose?

Above: *Mother (Adele Jergens) and daughter (Marilyn Monroe, right) in* **Ladies of the Chorus** *(1948). Mom was once married to a rich young man but was rejected by his family, who dissolved the marriage. She fears the same is about to happen to her girl: but Marilyn sings a couple of songs (including "Every Baby Needs a Da-Da-Daddy"), strips a little and soon wins over the snobs.*

Right: *A couple of years on, Marilyn won a prime part in* **The Asphalt Jungle** *(1950) as the naive young mistress of a middle-aged criminal lawyer, played by Louis Calhern with weary authority. She calls him "Uncle Lon" and he treats her as a delightful child, accepting her final weak betrayal of his alibi under police pressure as no more than par for the course. Marilyn had arrived.*

Below: *Three men set out to seek gold and find death instead, according to the traditional tale. In* **The Treasure of the Sierra Madre** *(1948) the three men are Curtin (Tim Holt), Howard (Walter Huston) and Dobbs (Humphrey Bogart). But Dobbs, despite his efforts to get rid of his partners, is the only one who actually dies, killed by Mexican bandits.*

Below: *Artist Eben Adams (Joseph Cotton) meets a girl (Jennifer Jones) in* **Portrait of Jennie** *(1949). She isn't all that she seems, however, having died long ago in a storm at sea. William Dieterle, with cinematographer Joseph August, experimented with tinted sequences to give a heightened romantic splendor to the rare encounters of the spiritual lovers. Delicate, refined Jennifer Jones surely found her proper atmosphere in this rarefied ethereal setting. Lillian Gish and Ethel Barrymore further added to the high tone.*

Elsewhere in 1949 films such as Robert Wise's brutally laconic **The Set Up,** about a fixed prize-fight, and William Dieterle's **Portrait of Jennie**, which gave an ideal role to the ethereal Jennifer Jones in a magical story of ghosts, time-traveling and love conquering death, were widely appreciated. Even if, by the beginning of the year, there were more than two million television sets in the United States, it seemed like a time of promise and development for the cinema.

As if embodying this buoyant mood, the genre that was doing worst – despite the encouragement of producers eager to ingratiate themselves with the HUAC investigators – was the anti-communist series, which included such dull and alarmist diatribes as **Iron Curtain**, **The Red Menace** and **The Red Danube**, while the genre that was surging forward by leaps and bounds was the musical. Obviously the public just did not care for awful warnings, and did want to be taken out of itself with singing, dancing, raw energy and color by Technicolor.

Foxy ladies

As usual, there were plenty of productions ready and willing to satisfy that need. At 20th Century-Fox a succession of luridly colored, artless but cheery musicals continued to emerge, without Alice Faye, who had retired from the screen in 1946, and without Carmen Miranda, who had moved on to fresh fields, but still with the irrepressible Betty Grable. She had just begun, in **Mother Wore Tights** (1947), a new and successful teaming with lanky song-and-dance man Dan Dailey and was to carry on as queen at Fox until finally replaced by Marilyn Monroe.

The studio had a constant supply of second-string musical ladies like June Haver and Vivian Blaine in reserve; one who did actually make real starring status, if only briefly, was Mitzi Gaynor, who made her debut in **My Blue Heaven** in 1950. Warners meanwhile had recently acquired Doris Day, and Paramount still kept up a series of brash semi-musicals starring Betty Hutton, who was introduced in **The Fleet's In** (1942) and had been barrelling her way through ever since. Paramount also had Bing Crosby, a law unto himself and perennially popular, whether on the road with Hope and Lamour or easing his way into the affections of each new generation with sentimental dramas like **Going My Way** and **The Bells of St Mary's**, or fully-fledged musicals like **Blue Skies, The Emperor**

Right: *Victor Schertzinger, who directed the first ''Road'' films for Paramount, sadly did not live to see the release of* **The Fleet's In** *(1942). A painfully shy sailor (William Holden, left) has to court a haughty nightclub singer (Dorothy Lamour) for a bet. He wins both bet and girl but his pal (Eddie Bracken) has a consolation prize – Betty Hutton (not shown) making her debut.*

Bottom right: *In* **The Bells of St Mary's** *(1945), the sequel to* **Going My Way** *(1944), easy-going parish priest Father Chuck O'Malley (Bing Crosby) comes into conflict with strict headmistress Sister, Mary Benedict (Ingrid Bergman, seated at piano) but a quick duet helps to break the tension. They come to terms and persuade a rich man to finance a new building for the school. Fate strikes at Sister Benedict, however, who contracts TB and is forced to retire. Yet all is not lost, for Father O'Malley's love saves the day.*

Below: *A typical 20th Century-Fox showbiz musical was* **Mother Wore Tights** *(1947). Vaudeville singer and dancer Myrtle McKinley Burt (Betty Grable) and her partner husband (Dan Dailey) are lovingly remembered by their younger daughter. The prolific Walter Lang directed.*

Waltz and **A Connecticut Yankee in King Arthur's Court**. Bob Hope sang, too, and had one of his biggest successes singing "Buttons and Bows" in **The Paleface**, co-starring Jane Russell.

Metro's golden musicals

The real home of the musical, particularly in the forties, was MGM. Arthur Freed was in charge of the grandest MGM musicals right through from the beginning of the decade, when he was promoted from associate producer on **The Wizard of Oz** to full producer, to 1949 and beyond. Freed may have dominated MGM's musical output, but there were two other producers at the studio, Joe Pasternak and Jack Cummings, who regularly made musicals, and several others who occasionally dabbled in the form.

The big stars and frontline directors usually worked with Freed, though not inevitably – every now and then a star like Judy Garland might be thrown to a producer like Pasternak for **In the Good Old Summertime** (1949), where she replaced the pregnant June Allyson. Freed, though, dominated because he had a superior grasp of what constituted the best, and how best to showcase it. The stars got to know and trust this, and developed a regular relationship with the so-called "Freed Unit", while unknowns, speciality stars like Esther Williams and others who were being brought on slowly or let down gently usually worked with Pasternak or Cummings.

Left: *In **The Paleface** (1948) Calamity Jane (Jane Russell) takes up with a nervous traveling dentist, Painless Potter (Bob Hope), while on an undercover mission and makes a marriage of convenience. After numerous adventures she decides that maybe she does love him after all. Meanwhile, he demonstrates his manhood by making passes at all the saloon girls **below left**. The song "Buttons and Bows" won an Academy Award. This was only Jane Russell's second (and last) forties film after **The Outlaw**; but never were two Westerns less alike.*

Below: ***The Good Old Summertime** (1949) was a rather brash Technicolor musical remake of Ernst Lubitsch's delicate romantic comedy, **The Shop Around the Corner** (1940). The tale of a shop manager and clerk who detest each other at work but unknowingly conduct an intense secret correspondence with each other was moved from Budapest to Chicago. Van Johnson and Judy Garland replaced James Stewart and Margaret Sullavan. But a dash of Hungarian atmosphere survived in the casting of S. Z. "Cuddles" Sakall as the store owner.*

Left and above: *The Pirate* (1948) is, for good and ill, one of the most artificial musicals in the history of cinema. Nothing is real, nobody tells the truth until the end, all is fantasy, deception, theater and studio. It is both stifling and liberating, both empty and packed with noise and colors. On a Caribbean island, a young girl, Manuela (Judy Garland), dreams of the fearsome pirate Macoco and believes she has found him when she meets a wandering minstrel, Serafin (Gene Kelly). She fantasizes a dance in which he challenges and awakens her emerging sexuality.

At the same time, the lesser MGM musicals were far from negligible. It is easy now to appreciate the relatively unsophisticated charms of Esther Williams in **Nelson's Daughter** and **On an Island With You**, or Jane Powell in **A Date With Judy** and **Nancy Goes to Rio**. Moreover, **Three Little Words**, a biography of Kalmar and Ruby produced by Jack Cummings, is not really much inferior to **Words and Music**, a biography of Rodgers and Hart produced by Arthur Freed.

But in the final analysis, what we remember as really special nearly always turns out to have come from Freed. The years 1948-49 were probably the peak of his achievement in fusing together the studio's array of creative, technical and artistic talents. Rouben Mamoulian's **Summer Holiday**; Vincente Minnelli's **The Pirate**, with Judy Garland and Gene Kelly; **Words and Music** with just about everybody; **Easter Parade**, which brought Fred Astaire out of premature retirement and teamed him with Judy Garland; **Take Me Out to the Ball Game**, which, under Busby Berkeley's supervision, at last gave Gene Kelly and Stanley Donen their choreographic and directorial chance; **The Barkleys of Broadway**, which reunited Fred Astaire and Ginger Rogers; and especially **On the Town** – all these were masterminded by Freed.

On the Town has frequently been tagged the key musical in the history of MGM, as important to the film musical as **Oklahoma!** was to the stage. This is hardly overstating the case: when Kelly and Donen let their three sailors (Kelly himself, Frank Sinatra and Jules Munshin) loose for 24 hours in New York, and brought them together with their matching girls (Vera-Ellen, Betty Garrett, Ann Miller), they created a new, freer world where song, dance and dialogue flow effortlessly into and out of one another. **On the Town** was not the first musical to shoot numbers in the open air, or to attempt an integration of this sort, but in no film previously had everything hung together with such ease, or been driven forward with such total, uninhibited energy. There were to be many successors in the fifties, some of which – **An American in Paris** (1951), **Singin' in the Rain** (1952), **The Band Wagon** (1953), and **Silk Stockings** (1957) – might be more to the taste of this moviegoer or that. But nowhere does one get quite so unmistakably the feeling of "Bliss was it in that dawn to be alive".

Hollywood was already in a difficult position, and was not to find it improved much in 1950, a year that added to mankind's store of experience the Korean War, the rise of Senator McCarthy and the explosion of the first hydrogen bomb. Many further indignities were in store. But for the moment **On the Town** is the perfect place for us to bow out of the forties, convinced every time we see it that movies were then better than ever, and that Hollywood – even on location in New York – was at that point immortal.

Top: *The climax of **Easter Parade** (1948) is, of course, the Fifth Avenue Easter Parade of, in particular, new hats ("In your Easter bonnet . . ."). Don Hewes (Fred Astaire) and his new vaudeville dancing partner (Judy Garland) are in love – and the music is by Irving Berlin. Who could ask for anything more?*

Above and right: *Even Peter Lawford, as Don's best friend, gets to perform "A Fella With an Umbrella" with Garland. But Astaire and Garland really scintillate in "A Couple of Swells". Ann Miller (not shown), as Don's ex-partner, also had a couple of good numbers.* **Easter Parade** *terminated Astaire's short-lived "retirement".*

Title Changes

British distributors changed the titles of many American films. Films mentioned in the book were retitled as follows:

U.S.		G.B.
The Amazing Mr Forrest (1939)	:	The Gang's All Here
Angel Street (1939)	:	Gaslight
The Brasher Doubloon (1946)	:	The High Window
Buck Privates (1941)	:	Rookies
The Clock (1945)	:	Under the Clock
A Dispatch From Reuter's (1940)	:	This Man Reuter
Farewell My Lovely (1945)	:	Murder, My Sweet (1945)
The Great McGinty (1940)	:	Down Went McGinty
I Wake Up Screaming (1941)	:	Hot Spot
Portrait of Jennie (1948)	:	Jennie
State of the Union (1948)	:	The World and His Wife
Take Me Out to the Ball Game (1949)	:	Everybody's Cheering
That Hamilton Woman (1941)	:	Lady Hamilton
White Savage (1943)	:	White Captive

PICTURE CREDITS

Cinema Bookshop contents page, 43, 45, 50, 53 bottom, 54-55, 70, 80-81, 82 top, 97, 115 **Joel Finler** half title, endpapers top right, 9, 13 bottom, 14, 15, 18-19, 21, 22-23, 36, 42-43, 51, 53 top, 55, 58-59, 68 73, 75, 77 centre, 86, 87 right, 88 bottom, 89, 92-93, 102-103, 104 top, 105, 109, 111, 117 **Flashback** 6-7, 10-11, 12, 27 **Ronald Grant** endpapers top left, bottom left, top middle, bottom middle, bottom right, 8, 10, 11, 13 top, 16-17, 19, 24, 24-25, 26, 28, 29, 30-31, 32-33, 33, 34-35, 35, 37, 39, 40, 56-57, 59, 60, 61, 66, 71, 74, 76, 77, 78, 82 bottom, 83, 84, 85, 88 top, 90, 91, 92, 94, 95, 96, 98, 98-99, 99, 104 bottom, 106, 107, 108, 110-111, 112, 113, 114, 116, 118, 119 **National Film Archive** title page, 20, 38, 41, 44, 46-47, 47, 48-49, 56, 62, 62-63, 64-65, 65, 66-67, 69, 72, 79, 87 left, 100

Many of the illustrations come from stills issued to publicize films made or distributed by the following companies: British National, Charles Chaplin, Columbia, Lester Cowan/Mary Pickford, Albert de Courville, Cecil B de Mille, Walt Disney, Samuel Goldwyn, Howard Hughes, International (Nunnally Johnson), Stanley Kramer, Liberty Films (Frank Capra), David Loew, Robert Hakin, London Films, Ernest Lubitsch (Alexander Korda), MGM, Lewis Milestone Productions, Paramount, Arnold Pressburger/Fritz Lang, Pyramid Amalgamated (R Murray Leslie), Republic, RKO Radio, David O Selnick, Twentieth Century Fox, United Artists, Universal International, Walter Wanger, Warner.

Multimedia Publications (UK) Limited have endeavored to observe the legal requirements with regard to the suppliers of photographic material.